Breaking into
the Boys' Club

The Complete Guide for Women
to Get Ahead in Business

BREAKING into THE BOYS' CLUB

Second Edition

MOLLY D. SHEPARD and **JANE K. STIMMLER**

with **PETER J. DEAN**

TAYLOR TRADE PUBLISHING
LANHAM • BOULDER • NEW YORK • LONDON

Published by Taylor Trade Publishing
An imprint of The Rowman & Littlefield Publishing Group, Inc.
4501 Forbes Boulevard, Suite 200, Lanham, Maryland 20706
www.rowman.com

16 Carlisle Street, London W1D 3BT, United Kingdom

Distributed by NATIONAL BOOK NETWORK

British Library Cataloguing in Publication Information Available

The Library of Congress cataloged the previous edition as follows:
   Breaking into the boys' club : 8 ways for women to get ahead in business /
   Molly D. Shepard, Jane K. Stimmler, and Peter J. Dean.
      p. cm.
   Includes bibliographical references.
   1. Businesswomen—Promotions. 2.Women executives. 3. Career development.
   4. Success in business. I. Stimmler, Jane K. II. Dean, Peter J., 1946– III. Title.
   HD6053.S417 2009
   658.4'09082—dc22

                                                          2008042248

ISBN: 978-1-58979-971-4 (pbk. : alk. paper)
ISBN: 978-1-58979-972-1 (electronic)

∞™ The paper used in this publication meets the minimum requirements of American National Standard for Information Sciences—Permanence of Paper for Printed Library Materials, ANSI/NISO Z39.48-1992.

Printed in the United States of America

This book is dedicated to the 72 million working women
in the United States who are committed to their jobs;
putting in long hours; juggling family, friends, and a multitude
of activities; investing in their individual success as well as that
of their companies—and trying to make a difference every day.

Contents

Acknowledgments

THE AUTHORS wish to thank the many women and men whose stories and experiences are included in this book, and who are trying to make the workplace a more balanced and equitable place.

We also acknowledge the wonderful women and men who have attended The Leader's Edge/Leaders By Design leadership development programs seeking to work together in collaboration and find fresh solutions. Our world of work will be a better place because of them.

As always, thanks to the family and friends who provide the support and encouragement to keep us going, and to our agent, Anne Marie O'Farrell, for all her good advice.

Confidential to Women

Alpha Dog

As my husband and I walk our dogs each morning, we often remark on the similarities between their behavior and the dynamics we see daily in corporate life. Our six-year-old male Maltese wanders this way and that until he notes that his two-year-old sister has found a favorite spot to do her "number one" business. At that point, he trots over to her patch of ground and claims it as his own by covering her scent with his own, clearly demonstrating the behavior of a dominant male.

In corporate life, as in the interaction of our dogs, the female is frequently deliberate and careful with her work, only to have the male instinctively diminish the accomplishment by claiming it, by ignoring it or maybe just by eradicating it. This is not true all of the time, but I bet it has happened to each of us women more than once. It is part of the game we play, and the better we understand the rules and how to work with men on equal terms, the more equipped we are to overcome the indignity of being invisible and to adopt tools that will let our work be seen, appreciated, and acknowledged.

Time and time again, I have heard women report that their ideas seem to fall on deaf ears in a meeting while a man may repeat her very idea later and get accolades for it. This happened to me a few years ago in a meeting I was leading. After we had discussed a problem, I offered a solution which was acknowledged, albeit not embraced. Ten minutes later, a man in the meeting suggested the same solution, for which he was applauded. I was stunned. Here I was, the chair of the meeting with enviable position power, and my idea was stolen from me. No one noticed except the other woman in the room, who quizzically raised her eyebrow at me. I thanked the gentleman for bringing up my solution again and regained ownership without being too aggressive. Upon reflection, I understood how careful a woman has to be under such circumstances. For me, the very narrow bandwidth of appropriate response—without sounding overly whiny or bitchy—is one all women must tread carefully.

The majority of women dislike office politics and want to be allowed to do their best work without being distracted by the game playing that occupies so much of our time. We want to be accepted as valuable team members, receive encouragement for our work, and be acknowledged for a job well done. Having an equal shot with the men at the next promotion, raise, or inclusion in an initiative would be nice, too. Most women I know enjoy working with men. After all, we have grown up with fathers and brothers, and we have always wanted to be included in their games. We have studied them close up and from afar. Now that we are in the workplace, we are excited and happy to be there, earning our way independently and managing the increased complexity of our lives.

The men, however, don't always seem to understand the value we bring to work. Women still feel excluded from important conversations that take place over lunch or a beer or on the golf course. We are either not invited or we may not be able to go because of other responsibilities. Men frequently, whether wittingly or unwittingly, will schedule meetings at 7:00 a.m. and at 6:00 p.m., which places extra burdens on women, the majority of whom still manage and coordinate household responsibilities. And, men sometimes appear to think they know what is best and even speak for women at meetings or in other discussions without checking with them first. I have sat in talent review meetings in major companies and have heard a man turn down a promotional opportunity for a woman, explaining that she would be unable to relocate her family or that she was unable to take on more work—*without conferring with her*!

As male leaders at work begin to learn more about our differences and ways of leadership, and understand our desire to be treated as equals while giving due consideration to all the other roles we play (mother, wife, chef, friend, networker, community champion, buyer, and consumer); hopefully they will be more patient with us and our seemingly hectic lives while appreciating our value at work. We like our busy lives and just want a fair shot at being a contributor!

Once Upon a Time

At the young age of twenty-three, I was appointed manager of a seven-person department in a company founded by three men. For seven years, though my team and I had one successful year after another, I was rarely congratulated for my hard work. However, we kept our noses down to our work and persevered. When I became pregnant, the bosses assumed that once my baby arrived, I would be unable to continue working, citing the fact that their wives had been unable to handle both motherhood and work. That made me determined to show them they were wrong and as a result, my two maternity leaves were, respectively, two weeks and four weeks so the men would not have time to replace me. I wanted to return to my job and prove them—and their wives—wrong.

These formative years of my career, in which I encountered various forms of prejudice and discrimination, led me to develop the resilience that has carried me forward to this day. I made a decision that in spite of the negative environment in which I grew professionally, I would rise above circumstances and push forward. Intuitively, I knew that there was a better way to operate in concert with the opposite sex.

Thus began my lifelong study of the tools and skills women need in order to survive the hurdles placed in front of them, intentionally or unintentionally, in the workplace. Though some of the women I worked with at my former company never got beyond their negative experiences, I chose instead to build two companies that were the exact opposite of the one I had started with. My companies were egalitarian and open in culture, and respectful of both women and men.

When faced with obstacles, some women respond with determination, resolving not to let their gender get in their way of achieving their goals. Others find the obstacles so distasteful that they leave the corporate world, sometimes forever. A woman business leader of African descent echoed my sentiments. She stated that her resilience was born of discrimination and difficulty. She learned from those, and went on to maintain her dignity and leadership in other venues that were more positive. Both of us vowed that we were never going to give away our self-confidence, and who we were, to men who had never learned to appreciate the value of the opposite sex. The possibility that men were consciously or unconsciously trying to get us to quit actually made us stronger and more convinced of our future success. Like me, she was not resentful or jaded, but both of us had developed antennae that made us aware of when we needed to assert ourselves or clarify our roles.

Perceptions

I have coached many senior women in my career, perhaps thousands. I have worked with them as they transitioned into new careers, counseled them on how to be more effective in their work styles, and advised them on becoming more powerful leaders. Through all my years in these different roles, I have been struck by the significant differences in how women view leadership and what motivates them to achieve great things on behalf of their companies. I have noticed, for example, that women are quicker than men to walk out the door and find jobs that they believe will make them happier. This happens when they feel that they are not appreciated, do not fit into their organization's culture, or are not being promoted like their male counterparts.

So, how can the workplace engage a woman's spirit and her energy so that she feels fulfilled, energized, and committed to the goals of the enterprise?

In my opinion, the single greatest factor leading to a woman's decision to move on is the loss of her self-confidence. Self-confidence is a very fragile thing and seems to take longer to develop in a woman. Women tend to be more vulnerable in this area, and confidence can easily be destroyed or eroded by circumstantial events. It is a woman's self-protective reaction to leave an environment she considers negative.

The second factor that seems to cause discontent in a woman is exclusion. Women have a unique ability to weave information, facts, and intuition into a plan of action or a strategy. When left out of the information loop by male colleagues, a woman notices and feels the pain of exclusion viscerally. If it continues, her work suffers, as does her self-confidence.

A third issue important to women is the need for feedback, positive or not, on a regular basis. This is because women are usually seeking perfection in what they do. If a woman does not get reinforcement for a job well done, her psyche reverts to self-criticism and questioning. If a woman's efforts are going in the wrong direction, she needs to hear this as well. In a constant search for self-improvement, this feedback can lead quickly to constructive changes.

A fourth key issue for women is the support of their companies. Women often feel the need to work harder than their male counterparts to prove themselves. And, due to the complexities of their lives, it is not uncommon for a woman to take work home, labor into the wee hours when the family sleeps, and find every means possible to go beyond expectations. If the company ignores this struggle and puts up obstacles to make her life more difficult, she will invariably choose family first and go elsewhere.

Finally, women have the need to understand the inner workings of their male colleagues' and bosses' minds. It is part of a puzzle that intrigues women at home and at work. We have an innate desire to figure men out so that we can be on the same wavelength. Let's look a little deeper and try to explain what women are really feeling.

Loss of Self-Confidence

Time after time, I have seen women who have allowed a male boss to treat them so poorly at work that they have lost their self-confidence. These women have entered the top ranks with résumés bursting with accomplishments, and have soon forgotten all the positive experience that gained them entry into the executive suite. The following story demonstrates how these feelings of inadequacy can cause a downward spiral. This can—and does—happen to men as well.

A woman I know—let's call her Laura—was recruited by a big pharmaceutical company. She brought fifteen years of successful brand management of some of the world's best-selling drugs. She had a $5 billion portfolio of drugs to manage and, in addition, was given the responsibilities of rebuilding a team that had been decimated by a former boss and renegotiating a critical strategic alliance that was in jeopardy. She was able to accomplish all of this in her first eight months on the job!

Yet, in spite of all her accomplishments, her boss belittled her, accused her of speaking out without consulting him, and began to cut her out of meetings. By the end of her first year, she had begun to doubt her own capabilities, and was convinced that she would never survive at the company.

This scene is, unfortunately, played out in companies every day. Colleagues often observe what is happening, but stay silent. Human resources may intervene, but only to take the superior's point of view. Higher level executives side with the man, often claiming that he is too valuable to discipline. When women are consistently ignored, verbally abused, or unacknowledged, they think about options such as dropping out, working on their own, or working for a smaller company. Women are willing to forfeit their "good" jobs for personal peace.

But if women want to stay in big corporations and receive the perks associated with the big jobs, they must find a way to survive. As they are marginalized, many women elect to leave voluntarily rather than be terminated, and justify their exits in the name of their families and inner harmony. In reality, they have been subtly coerced to leave and the companies are left to the men to run. Of course, each woman must do what is right for herself and her family. It is, however, important to understand the consequences of these decisions in a larger context. If women choose to leave their companies, the numbers of senior women grow at a slower pace, leaving management in the hands of the men and the culture unchanged.

Lessons Learned

Laura's situation is a complicated one. But how could it have played out differently? There are several factors that could have made a difference in the way the story ended.

1. Laura was, in the end, roadblocked because she didn't know the key decision makers. She hadn't spent enough time *building strategic relationships* with people who could have stepped up to her defense. This is something that women often forget to do in their pursuit of excellence. Having other key people in the company knowledgeable about her accomplishments and invested in her success would have made Laura less vulnerable.

2. She neglected to *ask for feedback* about her performance early on and was not *mentored* by anyone with the power and influence to bail her out. There are many sources of feedback. Human resources, peers, and even a respected person on her team could have provided some warning signs and advice. Selecting a well-placed senior executive as an informal mentor to her as she integrated into the company might have helped Laura.

3. Laura didn't recognize the very strong ego of her boss. She plunged ahead, making changes and strategic decisions, but neglected to share them with her boss. He was displeased with this because he felt pushed aside and became jealous of her growing power, especially with her team. To create a win-win situation, it would have been smart for Laura to *discuss her plans with her boss*, seek his advice, and then share credit.

4. Laura was seen as a leader who cared more about her team and its responsibilities than about the company overall. She wasn't regarded as a *team player*. Unintentionally, her enthusiasm to achieve results came across as territorial and set her apart from the senior leadership by demonstrating a lack of strategic vision.

In hindsight, Laura should have quickly gotten more traction in the company while she was working on her objectives. She also needed to know and appreciate a little more the male leadership style in order to collaborate more effectively with her boss, rather than appearing to compete with him. Finally, she needed to have respect for her place in the system. She was a large cog—but nevertheless only one cog—in the wheel.

The Importance of Self-Esteem

Earlier in this chapter, I talked about self-confidence, which is a key factor in the success of women and the area that pulls women down most. The fact is that when we women lack confidence in ourselves and our accomplishments, we show it. It shows in our tone of voice, our assertiveness, the ability to network with powerful people, and our interaction with male colleagues.

In my early career, I began to regularly question myself, especially before speeches and presentations. I would wonder, "What if they find out I am not what they think? If they look beyond the façade they will find the true me—an insecure, quivering mass of doubt and fear." This tendency to worry that people will see through their exterior shell straight to an insecure inner core is one that I see frequently in the women I coach. Does it really take years, as one of my colleagues suggested, for the inside of a professional woman to catch up with the outside? It seems so.

And, if a woman doesn't have a mentor, sponsor, or colleagues to believe in her, give her important feedback, and buoy her up in the difficult times, it will *never* happen.

What is this all about? I have asked hundreds of women this question and nearly all have said that they were raised to be "good girls" by well-meaning parents and teachers. They were supposed to be nonassertive, collaborative, and compliant. Even the girls who were raised by supportive fathers and mothers came up against prejudices in schools that countered what they heard as younger children. These messages are pretty strong at a time when we are developing our egos, and very difficult to turn around. But, if we want to rise up in our organizations, we must do exactly that.

Whatever the cause of our insecurity, it must stop! Women need to spend time on a regular basis reflecting on their positive attributes. They need to have a list of their accomplishments on the tip of their tongues and be able to recite them easily. They need to speak up in meetings and not allow others to bring up all their good ideas before they do. They need to increase their visibility throughout the organization, so that when an opportunity for a promotion or a project comes up, they are mentioned as candidates. And, they need to dress and act like leaders. These are all steps to building an executive image, which in turn attracts respect and inclusion into the inner circles of the organization. Men who feel trodden upon could do very well by following the same advice.

Self-esteem is a tricky thing to master. It starts with developing a full and honest recognition of who you are, what you have achieved, and what you want. As women, it is vital that we boost our confidence on a regular basis so that when we feel put down or unheard, we have a reservoir of strength to draw upon.

One of the most important exercises in my coaching work with women is to review their top accomplishments. When we list the events a woman is most proud of, she can then identify which skills she was using to accomplish each. As she runs through each accomplishment, the skills that she most relies on surface. These recurring skills serve as the basis of her leadership, and are the ones she should rely on to ensure ongoing success.

My Advice

Women, it is up to us to model new behaviors that will help men embrace our excellence, ease the pressure in the work environment, and ease tensions. We should also learn how to share information about ourselves—our aspirations and our strengths—that can help the (male) decision makers out there to operate with more insight.

> *Ask for feedback!* If you feel that something isn't clicking, then ask why. Ask a trusted colleague or another woman to watch your style in meetings and tell you what works and what doesn't work. Or, ask human resources for a confidential 360-degree review with colleagues to give you honest and straightforward feedback. You cannot change if you are lacking awareness.
>
> *Don't pout!* How many times do we tell our kids not to pout, and instead to come out of their rooms and talk about what is going on? If

you say, "What you did made me feel . . ." instead of hoping your boss or colleague will figure it out, you will inform men about what we need to be successful.

No whining! When we whine, our voices go up and become very shrill. Better to formulate your thoughts on paper, stay focused on what you want to achieve, and deliver the message in a clear and commanding tone.

Don't get mad, get better! When you receive feedback you don't like or understand from your male boss, take a breath and think about what the message really is. Does it have any merit? If it absolutely doesn't make sense, then ask for clarity and examples. If it still doesn't ring true, then pull out your list of accomplishments and remind him of your value and skills!

Give feedback to the men! When you see a clash in style, a misunderstanding, or a lack of appreciation of women's skills on the part of a male colleague, take the time to speak to him about it. This is your opportunity to educate him and perhaps open his eyes to the male/female differences and create more understanding.

Express yourself! Men will frequently brag about their exploits on the field, at home, and at work, while women tend to wait to be discovered. It's time for us to pick up our game and learn how to brag a little. Let your accomplishments filter through your conversations, ask for performance reviews regularly, and speak up when there is a promotion you deserve. Don't sit quietly and watch the person in the next office, who is more practiced in bragging, take the promotion himself!

Don't rely on looks! While beauty and great clothes will get you some notice, they will not get you respect. A reliance on the superficial will continue to reinforce that women are objects not to be taken seriously. Dress *and act* like a leader at all times. Determine your organization's leadership dress code and tweak or change your wardrobe accordingly. Your visual presentation is over 50 percent of your personal message, so if it sends mixed messages, it lowers your overall rating as a true professional.

Get guidance! Figure out the best person to guide you, advise you, and teach you the tactics and skills you need to grow. A good mentor is not always a kind mentor, so look for someone who will tell you the truth. And, you may have formal as well as informal mentoring relationships.

Periodic meetings with a well-placed executive can be very helpful in gauging your effectiveness.

Get out and about! Much of the real learning takes place outside of our offices—in the halls, at lunch with colleagues, and in the company of other professionals, competitors, and gurus in our fields. If no one knows who you are and what you have done, you won't get ahead.

Don't say it isn't so! Women who profess that their being a woman has had no effect on their careers are doing a disservice to other women whose experience is the opposite. If a woman has advanced to the highest levels of an organization with no negative experiences with the opposite sex, she is in the minority. Acknowledge the realities of most women and lend others a hand!

Women and men can do great things together. Some women have told me that women need to be less sensitive. Others feel that we need to believe in ourselves and know how good we are. I would also add that women need to support one another, avoid letting our emotions get us down, learn to be politically savvy, improve our communication style, and, above all, remember we are leaders!

Molly D. Shepard

Breaking into
the Boys' Club

What's Holding
Women Back?

N THE PAST FEW YEARS, a number of women have achieved leadership positions and broken barriers in the business world. There have been several new, high-profile female CEOs and COOs at Fortune 500 companies, and women have made other strides in business as well. These successes could lead to the conclusion that women are making substantial progress and, when we first wrote this book in 2005, we hoped that would be the case. However, while these achievements are significant, there continues to be a woeful shortage of women at the top and the pace of change is painfully slow, with little—and in some cases no—growth. Though women are attending college and graduate schools in record numbers and make up about half of the labor force, we are nowhere near parity with men. Facebook COO Sheryl Sandberg's book, *Lean In*, has brought this topic to the forefront once again. In the top 500 U.S. companies, about 50 percent of the "middle management" positions are held by women. But only 4.2 percent of those companies are led by women, women hold fewer than 17 percent of board positions, and just 14.3 percent of the executive officer positions are held by women, according to Catalyst.org research. And, to add insult to injury, on average, women still only make 77 cents for every dollar earned by men.

So, why do women still hold such a small proportion of the powerful, high-paying job positions?

Despite the number of talented and educated women in the workforce, we believe their lack of real progress up the ranks can be attributed to the persistence of ingrained male-dominated corporate cultures and the obstacles they present for women. A 2013 *Wall Street Journal* poll finds that 40 percent of working women say they have faced gender discrimination—a result that has not changed significantly from a 1997 survey! Many women, finding their work environment distasteful and seemingly intractable, prefer to opt out of the corporate world rather than try to adapt situations they see as unwelcoming and inflexible.

Though change is often difficult, frustrating, and uncomfortable, we are convinced that for women to make their marks, they must step out of their comfort zones and make crucial changes to their work styles—and perhaps to their styles at home as well. As greater numbers of women achieve authority and power, and more companies realize the benefits of maintaining their talent pool of top women, the cultural stalemate will, by necessity, change. A diverse workforce is the face of the future and, from a practical economic point of view, with half of the available talent being female and the market demographics increasingly diverse, companies will have to change to be competitive.

Women need to take a hard look at themselves and their corporate cultures, determine the best way to be successful where they are, and make adjustments to their approach. We believe this can be done while also maintaining their individual styles and identity. By identifying and dealing effectively with obstacles that are keeping them sidelined, women won't have to settle for unsatisfying careers or leave the workplace in frustration. Women can, instead, stay in the game, change the rules, and ultimately win.

In *Breaking into the Boys' Club*, we have identified the key areas that our research and experience have shown to be most problematic for women. These include *communicating* effectively and dealing with conflict, building *networking* relationships, *promoting* your accomplishments, being *politically savvy*, getting the most out of *mentoring and sponsorship*, maintaining *balance* in your life, and presenting yourself with *impact and presence*. In many cases, women know they should be taking steps in these areas but they just don't do it, even as they see their male colleagues using these techniques to succeed. Instead, women often complain about their situations and mull over the injustices they've experienced.

We cover each of these problem areas in depth, with insights and information on the common mistakes women make and tools to assess your own individual strengths and weaknesses. We provide *specific, actionable remedies* in each category to help you improve your skills and become more effective in your career, and include discussion and tips on work/life balance. If, after trying remedies, you still find that you're not making enough progress or are unhappy with your work, our book gives you the tools to keep your career on track by helping you understand where you are, pinpoint what's not working, and define the steps you can take to be happier and more successful.

Does the next story have a familiar ring?

Dan and Judy both went to solid liberal arts schools in the Northeast, earned B+ grades, and after graduation from NYU School of Law, each was hired by the same top insurance firm to work in the legal department. Years later, Dan is senior vice president and deputy general counsel, and Judy is an assistant counsel a couple of levels below Dan, stuck in a position going nowhere. Why did Dan succeed, and Judy fail to make it, in corporate America? Is he smarter? A better worker? Not necessarily.

The first day Dan walked into his new company, he was welcomed by his colleagues. A couple of the "guys" in his department, including the boss, took him to lunch and he got the scoop on the people, company politics, and the softball team. He was immediately included in meetings as well as the informal gatherings at lunch and after work. He was introduced to a number of people at higher levels, and felt a sense of instant camaraderie with his team. He got to know the right people, was well-liked, touted his accomplishments whenever possible, and was regularly promoted.

During Judy's first week, she went to lunch with two women in her department and heard about how their boss gave the best assignments to one of the men. They cautioned her about making sure she put in long hours, or her loyalty would be questioned. She came away convinced she had to constantly prove herself to others in order to get ahead. She went in early, stayed late, did great work, and developed a reputation as an expert in her area of law. After being passed over for several promotions, however, she understood that she probably wasn't going to go any further in her department.

Dan had a big advantage. He was immediately included in the corporate culture, and was given insight into the rules, the politics, and the people. From day one, Judy was trying to fit in and figure out what was expected while working long hard hours. She never felt she was on the "inside."

We have all heard women complain about being passed over in spite of their best efforts, just like Judy. Women are frequently at a disadvantage in integrating into the predominantly male corporate culture, which holds us back and leads to great frustration. The challenge of trying to break into the male-dominated culture, in fact, has become such an obstacle that women are leaving executive positions at Fortune 500 companies at *twice* the rate of men.

What's Happening Here?

It's hard enough for women to be taken seriously and be promoted to executive positions. Why would a professional woman who has worked long and hard to achieve her six-figure position voluntarily walk away from success? We decided to find out answers to these and other questions by conducting in-depth interviews with over one hundred senior executive women across the country who had done just that.

They told us their number one reason for leaving was: *a corporate culture that roadblocked their advancement.*

Many women felt their opinions were not valued and they had trouble being "heard" by senior management. The vice president of research at a multinational insurance firm said, "I need to feel engaged and connected with my work and the organization—to feel that I am contributing. I didn't get that feeling . . ."

They were excluded from important meetings, informal networks, and pipelines of information, which hampered their ability to do their jobs. A financial consultant told us, "I had skills of value that just weren't being used. When I expressed interest in a different kind of project or asked to join a task force, I was turned down."

The women expressed that they felt "underutilized" in their positions and needed to be motivated by more challenging work assignments. A senior manager at a big four CPA firm said, "I didn't feel challenged in my job. The company's idea of challenging me was to move me around in my unit and increase my workload, rather than giving me new and interesting types of assignments."

Others were concerned that the company did not reflect their ethics and values. The vice president of human resources for a media company felt, "My values were out of sync with senior management's values. I could no longer face my fellow employees and represent the company as fair and equitable knowing what I knew."

They didn't see any light at the end of the tunnel because they didn't feel they had a clear-cut career plan with the opportunity to gain exposure in different areas. The director of marketing for a large consumer goods company commented, "I was frustrated by a lack of career path. Even though I'm at a senior level, I still need a career path—I have to know there's somewhere to go."

In addition, the women interviewed expressed a strong need for a more balanced life with flexible working hours. The vice president of operations for a food services organization lamented that, "My boss saw no need to allow me to conduct work from home. I was willing to take a cut in pay—anything—to continue to work and also be there for my child. He said no to any flexibility in my work schedule."

Even when flexible options were available in their organizations, women were reluctant to participate for fear of being perceived as less committed to their positions. A director of special projects in the health-care industry observed, "It seems that family needs don't rank as high on men's lists as they do on women's. Senior women who are just as focused as men on their careers have the added pull and tug of their families and other relationships."

Over and over, the stories showed a picture of women fighting against corporate cultures that seemed to put up barriers that, in time, became so frustrating that the women gave up in their present companies and went elsewhere. Ninety percent of them changed companies or started their own businesses in their quest for a more welcoming culture. One woman surveyed reflected, "The difficulties in attaining a work/life balance raise the question: am I getting enough from this job to justify the conflict I'm feeling?" The women we interviewed answered with a resounding "no."

Biological Differences

Biological differences are key to understanding the ongoing tensions between men and women in the workplace. According to Louann Brizendine, in her 2006 book entitled *The Female Brain*, males and females see, hear, intuit, cognize, and sense differently due to different brain sensitivities:

> In the brain centers for language and hearing, for example, women have 11 percent more neurons than men. The principal hub of both emotion and memory formation—the hippocampus—is also larger in the female brain, as is the brain circuitry for language and observing emotions in others. This means that women are, on average, better at

expressing emotions, and remembering the details of emotional events (i.e., verbal agility, listening to learn more of the situation, empathizing in order to know what people are feeling, attending to others, respecting others). Men, by contrast, have two and a half times the brain space devoted to sexual drive as well as larger brain centers for action and aggression. . . . These basic structural variances could explain perceptive differences. . . . Men also have larger processors in the core of the most primitive area of the brain, which registers fear and triggers aggression. . . . This is why some men can go from zero to a fistfight in a matter of seconds while many women will try to defuse conflict.

These differences in brain structure explain, for example, why men are frequently more aggressive in their management styles while women often are more thoughtful in their decision making. Brain disparities lead to contrasting workplace styles and sometimes confusing interactions of the two genders as they work together.

Unfortunately, the "chain of command" work systems, which were designed and run by men, seem to perpetuate themselves and are very resilient to change. And, these systems are alien to most women, who don't have an understanding of, or affinity for, their rules of engagement. Women, instead, bring different skills that represent different ways of leading. At the root of these differences is simply diversity of thinking and behaving.

For example, women take a broader view on most issues. This can be called *web thinking* and entails:

- Gathering as much data as possible
- Weighing more of the variables and vantage points of stakeholders
- Considering more of the options and outcomes available
- Reviewing more points of view
- Recalling over and over those points of view to glean better insight
- Charting out more ways to see the next steps after a decision
- Tolerating ambiguity in conversation

Men think in a more focused way and give their attention to one thing at a time, tuning out everything else. Women are able to focus and still absorb the larger context around them using their two brain hemispheres. In conversations, women do "mental multitasking" while men laser in on the topic at hand.

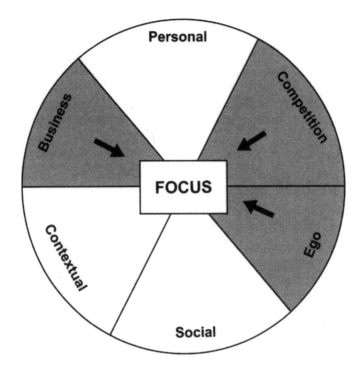

Conversations: Men

In conversation, men are focused on their business interests, the need to project their egos, and their basic drive to compete. Their concentration is single-mindedly on how to get the matter resolved or the project completed, and they are not thinking in a larger context.

Conversations: Women

Women, on the other hand, are able to attentively focus on what's being said, while still being attuned to many other things. In conversation, for example, women have the capacity to think about the business matter at hand, and at the same time, assess others as competitors or view them within a social framework. Women also say that though they may be deep in a work discussion, if they are interrupted by a phone call, request, or crisis, it's no problem. They can jump right back to their project without skipping a beat.

Simple biology supports this notion of more brain activity in the way information is processed by women. The differences in their physical brain

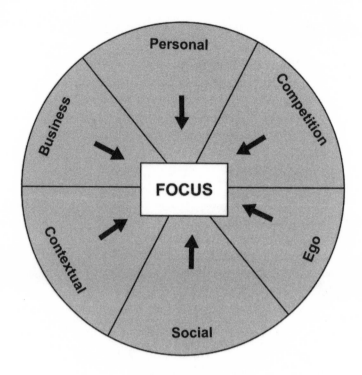

structure allow women to gather, integrate, and synthesize more diverse kinds of information, while men use a narrowly focused, compartmentalized process.

Here are the biological aspects, according to psychologist Karen Kahn Wilson, EdD, PCC, and consultant Steven Salee, MSW, MPA, that differentiate most women from most men:

1. The many connections in a woman's brain between the verbal and emotional centers enable them to access their feelings and the feelings of others.
2. Women have large numbers of sensory receptors located all over the brain that enable them to tune into sensitive nonverbal nuances.
3. Large quantities of the chemical oxytocin give women the ability to make positive connections with others.
4. The bundle of nerves called the corpus callosum connecting the left and right brains—which is thicker in women—enables women to multitask.

5. A woman's large prefrontal cortex is a distinguishing feature and allows her to assimilate large pieces of data and transform them into information.
6. Women's estrogen hormones help them to be more empathetic.
7. A woman's relatively small amygdala causes her to think, rather than act, in stressful situations.
8. Women have a comparatively large hippocampus, which allows them to remember details.

Making the Styles Work Together

We heard many women in the research studies we've conducted during the past few years complain about "the boys' club," and a large number of them are well justified. Complaining, however, will not take women to the next level—they can only achieve success by understanding and addressing their individual situations, and by taking action. Though we can be hopeful that the culture will change for the better, in the meantime it is wise to develop a clear understanding of the people and the politics at work in your company.

- What qualities are valued?
- Who's making the decisions?
- What skills are needed to get ahead?
- Who should you know?
- Who can affect your career?
- What is the most effective way to get things accomplished?
- What are the unstated rules and hidden barriers to women getting ahead?

Our book will help you analyze your culture and figure out where you fit in before you write it off. Are your ideas being heard by management? Are you connecting with the right people? Do you approach assignments in a way that gives the best chance for success? Do you volunteer for new projects and initiatives? Are you viewed positively by others? Do you look for opportunities for learning and advancement? Do you use your biological strengths to your best advantage?

Only after you have an understanding of your environment and yourself, and have carefully assessed your skills, strengths, and weaknesses, can you begin to overcome the corporate hurdles and be more successful. In order to get ahead in business, you need to be savvy enough to devote your energy to the places that count.

The woman who feels compelled to prove her worth by closing herself in her office, keeping her head down, and producing great reports, like Judy in the earlier story, is making a big mistake if she wants to advance up the ladder.

Instead, she should take time to develop key relationships, make important contacts, and understand her culture and its politics, like Dan. These are the skills beyond professional knowledge that take women to the executive ranks. As a high-level marketing executive told us, "Corporate America is a great training ground for some skills, but success at the higher levels is based more on political and other factors, not so much on the quality and quantity of your work. That's just expected."

Logic versus Reality: How Women Can Get Ahead

What *really* gets you ahead? Get ready to adjust your reality—it might not be what you think or were taught.

Logic tells you to:

- Work hard, put in long hours
- Always be on time and on budget with projects
- Have the best relationships with people you work with
- Be considered the expert in your area
- Take a minimum amount of time off
- Attend as many seminars as possible
- Go above and beyond your job description

But the reality is:

- Work smart, get known by those who count
- Promote your accomplishments
- Develop a network of contacts internally and externally
- Communicate your ideas effectively and think strategically
- Create a style with impact and presence
- Find a terrific mentor(s)
- Increase your community profile

If you do the things "that logic tells you," you will likely be a highly regarded employee and manager. These are positive attributes for anyone, and you can expect to be rewarded with periodic raises and praise for your work. They will not, however, put you in line for the top slots in your company unless you pay attention to "reality." If you work long hours and are great at what you do—*but the right people don't know you or your work*—you'll still find yourself roadblocked.

Take the example of Kristen, a talented woman who realized she had to make some changes to redirect her career. She had a senior staff position in a multinational consumer goods company, but was determined to get to a higher level. She knew that to get ahead she needed to jump to a line position, where the important decisions were made. In order to reach her goal, she resolved to make some necessary changes in her style.

Because she had not spent time building relationships with people around her, she had no real network of support. Kristen saw that her working style was insular and that she was still trying to prove to her colleagues how smart she was. She admitted that she had not given enough attention to her appearance and she needed to improve her image and look like an executive in order to achieve her goals.

Kristen started making some significant changes. She began scheduling lunch with colleagues and building a solid network. She developed a more relaxed working style, realizing that she was already highly regarded by others and didn't have anything to prove. People who had previously avoided her soon felt more comfortable with her. She also signed up at the gym, invested in a personal shopper, and starting looking more professional and feeling better about herself.

As it turned out, her self-assessment was on target, and her motivation and determination paid off. Not too long after, Kristen heard about a line position from one of her well-placed contacts in the company. She applied for the position, asked her colleague to lobby for her, and reached her goal of becoming a line manager. As time went on, she became part of the inner circle of decision makers and influencers at her company and eventually was promoted to senior vice president.

What was different? Kristen was willing to look at her herself openly and honestly, and to *change the habits that were getting in her way.* These changes—getting to know her colleagues better, toning down her attitude in meetings, refining her appearance, and stepping up to promote herself for a key job—led to developing better relationships, being included, gaining respect, and ultimately, landing the job! And, she didn't have to give up her identity or—heaven forbid—act like a man. Now that she was in a position of power, she realized that, over time, she could effect cultural changes that would make a difference by mentoring women coming up the pipeline.

In essence, it's a numbers game. As more women who are educated, trained, and getting closer to the senior ranks push through the barriers and into the executive suites rather than leave their positions in frustration, they will have the opportunity to make a difference. No longer will it be one lone woman's voice among fifteen men in executive meetings. More women will have the opportunity to bring to the table their expertise, viewpoints, and management styles. This will happen more quickly in some industries, such as the health-care and financial service sectors, where there are more qualified women in the pipeline, than in the manufacturing industry, for example. Yet, as the number of senior women executives increase, and greater numbers of corporations recognize the talent that women bring to the workforce, we believe that the corporate landscape will move more quickly to adopt change. We hope the information and advice offered in our book will help you reach your goals and effect positive change for all women.

Did You Know?

Women dominate consumer markets. Women purchase, or influence the purchase of, over 85 percent of all consumer goods, such as home furnishings, cars, and electronics, according to *BusinessWeek.* They make over 80 percent of all health-care decisions, and purchase 93 percent of all food and over-the-counter pharmaceutical products. Yet only twenty-one (that's 4.2 percent) of the Fortune 500 companies—the companies that produce and manufacture many of these products—have female CEOs, and only 16.6 percent of the board seats are held by women.

Women comprise 46.9 percent of the labor force. Women's representation in the U.S. labor force hasn't changed dramatically over the past twenty years. However, Catalyst reports that they have jumped from holding about a third of the managerial positions to about 51 percent. But women comprise only 14 percent of the officer-level positions in Fortune 500 companies, up from 9 percent a decade ago. They are a mere 6.7 percent of the top earners, and on average make only 77 percent of what men earn.

There are estimated to be 7.8 million women-owned businesses. That's up from 6.4 million almost twenty years ago, reports Catalyst. And, the number of women-owned companies with one hundred or more employees has increased at nearly twice the growth rate of all other companies. Yet, women get less than roughly 6 percent of the $30 billion venture-capital pie.

Globally, less than a quarter of senior business positions are occupied by women. The figure for businesses with no women in senior management positions is 34 percent, according to Grant Thornton. Top countries for numbers of women in management are Russia, with 46 percent, followed by Botswana (39 percent), and Thailand (39 percent). Lowest in women managers: India, Germany, and Japan (at, respectively, 14 percent, 13 percent, and 15 percent). The average percentage of women on boards in Europe as a whole is only 12.8 percent. Recognizing the need for improvement, Norway, and more recently Spain, have required companies to fill 40 percent of corporate board seats with women.

So, the compelling question examined in this book is: *why aren't more women breaking into the boys' club?*

1

Deliver the Right Message
Communicate Clearly and
Get Your Ideas Heard

ALLY, WHO IS based in New Jersey as head of a project team at a well-known international consumer goods company, recently told the following story. She and a male coworker regularly met to share stories and information. During one of their lunch conversations he asked her about a recent high-level project meeting she'd attended in Atlanta. She started to launch into the story in detail, beginning with her trip out to the meeting, and then abruptly stopped.

"Wait—before I go on—do you want the woman's version, with all the details, or the CliffsNotes—the man's version?"

He thought a minute, then replied, "The woman's version. I'm really interested."

They both laughed, recognizing the truth of that statement, and she went on with her detailed story. She began by telling him about how she and their colleague from another department traveled together and were held up by a flight delay, which made them arrive two hours late to the first meeting. She continued with particulars about the meeting participants and who seemed to be aligned with which "team." She'd been out to dinner with the group and shared the juicy stories one of their Chicago counterparts had told her. Twenty-five minutes later, she ended by describing the next phase of the project and how she felt about the pros and cons of working on it.

One of the many ways men and women are different in their communication styles is in the way they report information. Women like to talk about people, setting, context, drama, and inner meaning. Men usually skim the surface, touching on current events, sports, and the stock market. As we'll later discuss, the detailed reporting style of women is frequently seen by men as "rambling." No wonder in a survey conducted by The Leader's Edge, both the women and men executives polled agreed that the two sexes communicate differently. It is important for women to understand how their styles of communication are perceived by others. If women do not gauge their style and make necessary adjustments, corporate doors can close on them without their even understanding the reasons.

Women's communication styles are often misconstrued and perceived differently from men's. This greatly impacts on their ability to be heard, be included, get their ideas across, and become leaders in the business world. A woman who responds to being interrupted constantly by her male colleagues by interrupting *them* can be seen as pushy, but a woman who politely waits in a meeting to be called on and never speaks up is seen as weak. Women must discard some of the polite behavior learned in childhood that doesn't work in the corporate world, such as: *wait to be asked* your opinion, *don't boast* about your accomplishments, *raise your hand* and be recognized before speaking, and *don't dominate* the conversation.

Why Communication Is a Catch-22 for Women

Have you ever been complimented for being a good listener? Or told that you have the knack of including everyone's opinions and thoughts in a group setting? While you may think of these traits as positives—and in many situations they are—they don't necessarily translate that way to the corporate world. The chart on the following page lists a number of characteristics of women's communication that are in this "catch-22" category.

Relationships

Heads turned as a well-known attorney walked into the Ritz-Carlton's restaurant at lunchtime. Ben stopped at several tables, moving quickly as he spoke to a number of people, and had several "significant" business conversations in a short period of time. Though his interactions consisted largely of

The "Catch-22" Corporate Communication Chart

Women's traits	Which men see this way
Women are good listeners.	Many men perceive this as passive.
Women politely let others speak first.	Women are not seen as real participants.
Women raise their voices in meetings to be "heard."	Women are often told their style is too aggressive.
Women like to solicit others' opinions and get feedback.	Many men see this as a form of indecisiveness.
Women are "relationship developers."	Women's deep conversations are viewed as a waste of time.
Women are serious about their work.	Women can be seen as lacking a sense of humor.
Women use body language and facial expressions to encourage speakers.	Women's behavior can be misinterpreted as agreement.
Women show sensitivity in their language and management behaviors.	Women can be seen as soft and emotional.
Women give detailed reports.	Many men see women's reporting as rambling.

handshakes, pats on the back, and not much more than "How are you, Bill? Good board meeting yesterday! What did you think of Joe's proposal?" or "Hey Mike—great game on Saturday! Let's get together soon and talk about the Stanford case," he connected with the people he knew. He accomplished a great deal in less than fifteen minutes, making more than ten business contacts. He clearly was a master of this type of communication.

Women take relationship building seriously by establishing meaningful connections through significant and lengthy conversations. If we don't have what we consider a substantive conversation with an individual, we may not feel satisfied with the interaction. Why is this problematic? Longer conversations slow women down in today's fast-paced business climate and, as a result, we often have smaller, closed networks, while men, who spend less time in conversation, tend to have large networks, which benefit them by giving them more diverse and wide-ranging information. They do this by having many relationships through various points of contact—clubs, professional and civic organizations, sports activities, and so on. This allows them to bring information back to their company and demonstrate that they have broad knowledge about who's doing what in terms of the competition and general business community.

In the same situation as Ben, most women would have stopped to chat with the first person they knew and had an in-depth conversation, leaving no time for making further contacts before lunch. While this would clearly be a more satisfying exchange for the woman, it would not meet the business objective of establishing a broad network. While women's relationships are often deep and caring, they usually have fewer of them, more centered around friendships, and this hampers their networking in the business world. In order to be as effective as possible, women need to make the distinction between business and social behavior and ramp up their networking skills.

Listening

Women are perceived as better listeners than are men, and while this can be an asset, it is often viewed as a weakness by men in a meeting situation. It makes the woman appear tentative, passive, and without a strong opinion on what is being discussed. And, if she waits until the meeting has ended to share a great idea with a coworker, she has, in essence, wasted her good idea by not revealing it to the group. She may even produce a negative reaction—"Why didn't she speak up when we were all together in the meeting?" It's vital to stay focused on the discussion and, instead of keeping your thoughts to yourself, speak up. That way, colleagues know that you are involved in the discussion and hearing the important issues. Eighty-three percent of executives surveyed by The Leader's Edge said that women are better listeners than their male counterparts. This is a trait women need to use to their advantage.

Tip: Jump In

When in a meeting or conversation, jump into the discussion early to ensure you are a part of the dialogue or you may feel awkward later on. Take advantage of your good listening skills and seize on something you've just heard, formulate your thoughts quickly, and respond. You'll be seen as an involved and thoughtful member of the group.

Getting Heard

Leigh, who is vice president of human resources at a manufacturing firm, felt she wasn't being heard in her executive team meetings and took action to remedy the situation. The meetings were held in a large room with everyone seated at a long conference table and Leigh frequently ended up sitting on the same side of the table as the CEO. She realized that by not being in his line of sight she was invisible, and so she made an effort to sit on the opposite side of the table, even if it meant arriving early to claim her seat. She also noticed that no one stood up to speak and decided to take a chance. When she was ready to contribute, she stood right up, saying, "I hope you don't mind—I thought you would hear me better," and delivered her report. She stood out and her approach was well received. She very quickly found herself called upon more and more for her opinion and advice.

Another story on this topic is one that occurred during a subcommittee meeting of the board of directors of an organization. The group was discussing how to select new candidates for the board. The chair, a woman, proposed an analysis of the current members of the board to determine what kinds of industries and skills were missing, so that they could look for candidates who could fill those criteria. The group acknowledged the idea and continued the discussion.

About ten minutes later, a male board member who is a well-known community leader spoke up and said, "I have an idea. Why don't we do an analysis of the board membership and determine what we're lacking in terms of industries and skills?" One of the other men immediately turned to him, saying, "That's a great idea! Let's move ahead on it. How should we get started?"

The chair was stunned—it was as if they hadn't heard the same great idea ten minutes ago. She couldn't believe that one of the senior men in the group had just adopted her idea as if it was his—and no one remembered she'd said it. She took action and said, "Thank you for bringing up my idea again. I agree it's a good one, so let's proceed." Though careful to be respectful of her fellow board member, she reminded the group where the idea had originated. A wink from the only other woman in the room let her know she "got it."

Tip: Get Heard in a Group

In order to get your voice heard, use your ingenuity to find the best way to get into the discussion. If you're in a crowded room, stand up to project your words. If you have a soft voice, speak more loudly than usual.

If the conversation is coming fast and furious, seize on a break in the action to speak up. Your self-confidence will go a long way in getting your message across.

Sounding Strategic

In a meeting, before getting bogged down in minutiae, make clear statements about how the project fits into the business strategy of the company and overall vision of your organization. Make it clear that you have the big picture in mind, and use the who-does-what details to support the strategy, not drive it. Women find themselves getting caught up in details and, because of this, frequently are not viewed as strategic thinkers. Instead of talking about a vision for the future, or the global impact of a project, women often talk about the specific steps needed to solve a problem or drive an initiative forward. While this is a practical approach and the details will need to be thought out to move the project ahead, don't allow yourself to be pegged as simply an "implementer." Be conscious of conveying that you are a "big thinker" as well.

Assertiveness

Behavior that is routinely considered "appropriately assertive" in men can be seen as "unpleasantly aggressive" in women. The answer is for women to be assertive, not aggressive. It's a matter of degree and is determined by tone of voice, level of voice, and attitude. Because it's such a subtle difference between the two, women should be mindful of the distinction. While it is always appropriate to speak out confidently and with substance, women *can* sound shrill to the male ear, so there's an invisible line that shouldn't be crossed.

Some of the cardinal rules to "assertive communication" include never challenging the leader of the group in public, never embarrassing anyone, and never personally attacking someone. A director of marketing who was working on her assertiveness and making progress took it one step too far. She criticized her boss at a meeting—and paid dearly for it. He wanted to table a subject and she wouldn't let it go, finally accusing him of not openly addressing the issue. This caused irreparable damage in their relationship and he lost confidence in her.

Another rule is never to make it personal. In a discussion about reducing costs, a special projects director at a university who was angry at her coworker's position told him in a huffy tone of voice, "You always refuse to cooperate even though you're overstaffed and always have been." It was the wrong tactic because it was not professional and—maybe even worse—it sounded whiny. As a member of the executive team, she would have been more effective if she'd described the company's urgent need to cut costs and the possibility of layoffs. Later, she could have taken her coworker aside and expressed her thoughts on a more "personal" level.

Tip: Keep Your Cool

Never allow yourself the luxury of anger, no matter how "hot" the discussion gets. Instead, control your emotion so it doesn't interfere with your message. Keep your anger in check by preparing ahead of time for your meeting and knowing the challenges you may face. Think about the issues and visualize possible arguments that will be made. This way you'll be able to plan your response instead of simply reacting.

Soliciting Opinions

Women's styles favor inclusion in decision making. When leading meetings, women often ask questions and seek everyone's opinion before making a decision. In a one-on-one or social setting, this is a positive because it makes individuals feel included. In a meeting, however, the same behavior can be seen as evasive or passive or "un-leaderlike." It is both necessary and important to receive the input of others in a meeting, but this must be done with authority and purpose.

State your position on the subject being discussed at the beginning of the meeting. If you've already come to a conclusion, you can begin by telling the group, "I'm leaning in this direction, but I'd like to know if anyone has something to add or feels strongly." On the other hand, if you haven't made up your mind, you can say, "I'm really pretty open on this and would like your input." Don't ask for opinions when they won't be valued or the group may end up feeling patronized or frustrated. Control the situation and set a time limit on discussion. As the meeting leader, conclude the meeting with a summary of what has occurred and the next steps to be taken. An example is, "Thanks to all of you for your suggestions. We've explored each of the possible directions for the project and have decided to pursue Plan B. We've also discussed responsibilities, so unless there are further questions, let's meet next Tuesday to discuss our progress. I'll send out a confirming e-mail."

Formal Style

As women rise up the corporate ladder, research shows their style becomes increasingly formal. They use formal meetings rather than informal settings to get and give information. However, this behavior plays into the criticism that women are unfriendly, aloof, lack a sense of humor, and are not part of the team. An investment banker told us, "Most of the senior women in the company don't hang out after work with the guys. I'm not sure how much that affects our career—it does set us apart."

The more a woman does to be "one of the group" the more likely she is to be included in the information loop. Laura, the executive vice president of a large financial institution, noticed that all the other members of the executive team who reported to the president played golf together regularly. Laura took golf lessons (eventually becoming an excellent golfer) and joined in this group activity, which put her into the informal communication loop and cemented her as "one of the team."

This can be accomplished in many ways—*you don't have to take up golf!* But it is important to observe where and how the informal conversations are taking place, and determine the best way to be included. Do the "players" who matter go to lunch together? If so, make the gesture of asking one of the group members to have lunch and you may eventually work your way into the group. Do they gather for coffee first thing in the morning or a drink after work? Saunter into the coffee room and join in the chitchat, or stop for a quick drink (even if it's club soda) after work. After doing some detective work you can see where you might fit in and then try to make inroads.

Maintaining a distance through a more formal work style is safer in some ways and can serve to shield a woman. While women are, on one hand, often excluded from informal activities, when they *are* invited they may find themselves subject to scrutiny, with people (especially men!) tending to notice the way they're dressed and how they conduct themselves. In spite of this dilemma, you will benefit by becoming a part of the informal network. As more women participate, it will become standard operating procedure rather than an opportunity to take shots and fuel gossip.

Humor

Banter is the way men relate to one another, and kidding, teasing, and jokes are staples of the workplace. When a woman is included in the joking, it is often a sign that she is considered part of the group. A vice president at a bank who had started to be included in the kidding and digs by her coworkers wasn't sure whether this was good or not. Her boss assured her this probably indicated she was "one of the guys," which meant they felt comfortable and accepted her.

When women don't participate, this can isolate them, alienating them from the connections made through this type of contact. Resist the impulse to get on your high horse and disparage harmless kidding or even a prank here or there. Women should show their sense of humor, through actively participating or showing appreciation for the banter or joke. The simple act of smiling or laughing goes a long way in generating goodwill and establishing rapport, whether one-on-one or in a meeting or presentation. You can be human, and still be seen as professional. We all know people who go overboard on humor, telling jokes that are not funny or showing insensitivity to others. In those instances, no one would be blamed for not participating.

Planning for Meetings

Elizabeth is the new sales and marketing director for a product line of a large chemical company. She is ready to begin leading an important meeting to discuss the latest product trends and the need for a major market research project. She has prepped her boss, who is supportive of the project. Her objective is to get team consensus on her proposal for the research. As she scans the meeting room, noting that everything is in place, she feels confident that the meeting will run smoothly and have the desired outcome. Why?

Planning for a Meeting: Leader

- She went over the meeting room arrangements last week.
- She has confirmed meeting attendance with an e-mail to everyone.
- She has spoken with colleagues and found out what's happened with the product line over the past few years.
- She understands the focus of the company and knows where her product fits into the mix.
- She has developed thoughtful responses for all objections she anticipates hearing.
- She has touched base with the key participants, including the new product development people, and because her argument proved persuasive, they now support her recommendation.

- She has met with the financial person who had concerns about the reallocation of resources to support the project, and he now understands the advantages of doing so and has agreed to her plan.
- She has an agenda that permits her to achieve her objectives within the set time limit.
- She has prepared her presentation and handout material to crisply summarize the key information.
- After a final run-through last night, she feels self-assured in her leadership of the meeting.

Tip: Be a Strong Meeting Leader

Establish your presence as a leader when you enter the room by greeting each person individually and looking them in the eye. As you begin the meeting, speak in a clear, steady, authoritative voice, stick to your agenda, and stay within your time parameters. Make it a point to recognize all members of your audience and to "read" them periodically to make sure you're on point.

Planning for a Meeting: Participant

Now let's look at the participant's side of the meeting. Jackie, a manager from the product development area who wants to put forth ideas and contribute, also has some planning to do. She has a stake in the outcome of the meeting, and wants to be sure she has covered her bases thoroughly. How?

- She has met with Elizabeth prior to this meeting to discuss the issues.
- She has familiarized herself with the meeting agenda.
- She has prepared an outline of points she wants to cover at the meeting.
- She heads to the meeting room a few minutes early in order to assess the room, decide where to sit, and place her belongings to reserve a desirable seat.
- She had a chance to touch base briefly with Elizabeth before the meeting begins.
- She contributes her thoughts almost immediately, maintains eye contact with everyone in attendance, and is a key part of the discussion group.
- Afterward, she walks back with a couple of coworkers and they all discuss their reactions to the decisions made.

■ She is pleased with the result and sends an e-mail to Elizabeth to follow up on a couple of points.

Being prepared is an important way to establish a leadership style. To do this, you'll first want to have a mental checklist of the steps to go through *before* the meeting, as Elizabeth did. Use the following checklist before you lead your next meeting to make sure you've covered all your bases.

Pre-Meeting Planning Checklist

☐ Review who will be attending the meeting and what their interest is in the outcome.

☐ Determine the history behind the meeting agenda—has this topic been discussed previously?

☐ Meet with the participants to review their thoughts and ideas, listen to the pros and cons, and incorporate them into my strategy.

☐ Find out where "the boss" stands on the issue!

☐ Check out the meeting room size, seating arrangement, etc., and decide where I will position myself in the room.

☐ Prepare my information and do the necessary research.

☐ Identify possible points of opposition to my ideas and determine how to effectively deal with them.

☐ Rehearse my "pitch" or presentation, and run it by a trusted colleague.

Style Differences between Women and Men

An important tool used in coaching executives is a 360-degree colleague interview and feedback process. The interviews are conducted by experienced coaches and include individuals, both men and women, who work with the person being coached—peers, subordinates, and managers who have observed her leadership and communication styles. The answers are integrated into one report, so that while the participant gets straightforward feedback, the identities of the respondents are not revealed. They are asked a series of questions about the participant such as:

- What are her major strengths and skills?
- What do you consider areas of development for her?
- Describe her leadership style.
- What is her communication style—one-on-one and in a group?

When the men participating in a 360 are asked to comment on their communication with the women, a curiously consistent phenomenon occurs. The men's response is frequently, "I don't understand her." And, when probed, comments range from, "She's not direct," to "She rambles," to "She's not strategic." These are surprisingly harsh words for very senior women who have seemingly had no problem in the communication area and in getting promoted to their present position.

Tip: Zip It!

Think about the best way to phrase your message, say it clearly—and then stop talking. Your silence will enable you to gauge your listener's reaction, process it, and respond in a more productive way. Silence can be a powerful tool that can help you communicate more clearly.

Men often have difficulty relating to a woman's style of communication. One law firm director said, "I think men just feel more comfortable with someone like them—they can talk sports and use sports language and metaphors." However, often a woman's style can be an asset. A woman physician was the only woman in a large practice of sixteen doctors in Chicago. The men treated her in a somewhat disdainful manner and made snide comments about her style with patients. Since she took extra time to listen and was more consultative (read here: chatty), they decided maybe she just wasn't as sharp as they were. She endured this until the process changed and the patients were able to choose which physician they saw. Guess who they chose? Her practice thrived while the men's declined—so much so that they started discussing the possibility of taking courses in better communication.

While men may not be comfortable at first with women's communication styles, the women surveyed tell us they often feel the same way about the men they work with. A woman in commercial real estate told us, "At management meetings where I was the only woman, anyone who failed to meet his target numbers was berated and it was clear you weren't supposed to come to their defense. I was shocked by this behavior. It's a different way of operating, certainly not my way, and I felt it was a gender-specific pattern." It is clear that women react very differently than men to this angry type of behavior and take it to heart. The CFO at a financial company had this perspective: "In budget meetings, for instance, men will be vigorous, even hostile in their discussion. They'll bloody each other, then go have a beer together. We women leave that same meeting confused and upset."

The question is: how can women deal with a tough business style without taking it personally?

A director at an educational consulting firm told the story of being at a combative meeting during which a male peer was yelled at and embarrassed by their boss. After the meeting, my friend spoke to her coworker to find out how he was feeling about the incident. He turned to her and said, "Oh, that. He's a total jerk!" He had turned the incident 180 degrees and instead of taking blame, he had placed it squarely on his boss and moved on. Another man, a CEO of a bank, told me that when he's in a meeting in which someone becomes angry at him, he first thinks about what's really causing the problem, recognizing that it may be a bigger issue than the one being talked about. He then tries to take a role in calming things down. He is able to objectify the situation and deal with it rationally. Though easier said than done, these are valuable insights into how to deal with such situations. It's important to learn to be more resilient and to take things less personally if you want to have less stress in the workplace.

Tip: Don't Make It Personal

*When a boss or coworker gets angry, try not to take it personally. Instead of thinking about how **you** feel, put your focus on the person who is angry and try to figure out **his or her** motivation. What is really causing that person to be out of control? Is there a way to calm him or her down? Is this behavior a part of his or her persona? Put the blame clearly where it should be—with him or her, not with you!*

The way women view and react to anger or sarcasm can isolate them from others, specifically men. When a woman takes angry office behavior too seriously or gets "emotional" about it, her male colleagues, who are accustomed to shrugging it off, often feel uncomfortable and may want to avoid the situation. If this happens, the woman can lose potential allies and, eventually, attention to her ideas and her support base.

Are You Getting Your Ideas Across?

Consider the following two business scenarios. Imagine that there is a meeting of division members in a consumer goods packaging company to discuss new ideas for expanding the product line. A female manager begins speaking . . .

> **Scenario #1:** "I'm not sure about this one. You may not like it but . . . I have this idea about expanding our drink cup line into a new market. I think the sales reps I've talked to are pretty excited about it. But it would require buying some new equipment. You're probably not happy to be hearing that . . . but I've run the numbers and I think we would probably break even in less than a year—and after that, we would be close to turning a profit. I think it's something we should consider."

> **Scenario #2:** "I have an idea to share with you for expanding the drink cup line. George, John—I bounced this off of you the other day. It works this way: A new piece of equipment would allow us to wrap the cups and sell them to the hotel market—a segment we've never been able to reach. The numbers show that even with the cost of the new machine, the increased volume would allow us to break even in six months and double production in a year. In fact, let me pass around the numbers so we can take a look at them . . ."

How do *you* react to these distinctly different styles of communication? Did you notice that Scenario #1 is filled with discounting words and phrases, while the speaker in Scenario #2 sounds authoritative, knowledgeable, and confident? Speaker #2 used no discounting words, delivered her message in a positive and cogent way, involved her team members, and shared information. This is a woman who will be heard and respected for her ideas.

Do You Use These Words in Business?

Many women are not even aware of how they use phrases and words that soften their message. Some examples are:

Do you think?	Could I?
I'm not sure	What if I?
Maybe	I would like to
Perhaps	Probably
Possibly	You might not agree, but
If you don't mind	Almost certainly
If I might	More than likely
Would it be okay?	I guess
I think	

To become attuned to this, try counting the number of times you hear these words and phrases. (I recently listened to a presentation by a woman who used "I think" twenty-six times!) Replace the above with *stronger words and phrases*:

My point is	I recommend
My idea is	My suggestion is
The numbers show	After reviewing the report
Research indicates	I feel strongly that
I recently observed	My experience suggests
Let's go forward	

Once you learn to hear the discounting phrases you use, *think about how you would replace them with more effective language like this!* When you do, you will be heard and respected for your ideas—the same ideas you may be going nowhere with now.

How to Improve Your Style

To get better at this, you need to continually evaluate your style during your workday. Grab a notebook!

Self-Analysis

If you are analytical and tend to remember the details of situations, you can assess your style by thinking about your behavior and language in recent meetings or conversations, and analyzing your results.

Step 1

Review recent interactions, evaluate whether they were positive or negative in terms of communication, and think about how and why. Did you feel you were being understood? Did you get irritated or frustrated? Did your voice change in tone? Was your message clear?

After you've run a meeting or given a speech, make a list with two columns: one positive, one negative. List what you did and did not do well. Which is longer?

My Most Recent Meeting or Speech

What I Did Well: **What I Didn't Do Well:**

_____   _____

_____   _____

_____   _____

_____   _____

_____   _____

Step 2

Reflect on a very positive meeting or discussion you've led and think about what you did to make it a success. Did you understand people's personal and professional agendas? Did you prepare a meeting agenda? Did you keep the interaction lively? Did you start and end on time? Did you ask for input? Did you conclude with next steps? Did you set up an action plan and follow up? Write down the word "success," and list the things you did best when you led your last meeting!

Success!

What I Did Best to Lead:

_____

_____

_____

_____

_____

Step 3

Now, think of a meeting or discussion you've been a part of and think about what you did to add to its success. Did you get to the meeting in time to grab a good seat and say hello to colleagues? Did you know the agenda and prepare for the discussion? Did you actively participate? Did you listen carefully to understand people's views? Did you contribute to the discussion?

Write down the word "success," and list the things you did best in your last meeting!

Success!

What I Did Best to Participate:

_____

_____

_____

_____

_____

Step 4

Think back to an unsatisfying conversation with your division head or manager. What went wrong? Did you use discounting language? Were you rambling because you were unprepared? Was your timing poor? Did he or she feel attacked or undercut? Did you feel attacked—and if so, why?

Be honest and make a list of improvements needed. Keep it handy, refer to it, and start making changes!

Improvements!

What I Need to Change:

_____

_____

_____

_____

_____

As you go forward, keep your lists in a notebook and add to them after meetings and interactions. Pay more attention to your communication and language so you can monitor your progress. This self-analysis method requires having a good memory and being honest with yourself.

Audio

It may give you a jolt to listen, but you can't argue with what is on tape! A good way to get realistic feedback is to pick an appropriate meeting and ask your fellow participants if, instead of taking notes, it's okay with them if you tape the meeting. You'll want a tape recorder that can be put on the conference table to pick up the sound in the room. This works especially well if you happen to be running the meeting, because you'll get the best information in addition to having a valid reason for taping. Before the meeting starts, try speaking from different points in the room. Can you hear yourself? Will you need to speak louder at one end of the table? As you replay the tape after the meeting, ask yourself:

- How do you feel about what you're saying? Are you on message or do you stray from your point?
- How are people reacting to you? Are people listening or are they interrupting you? Are they treating your ideas with respect?
- What about the sound of your voice? Is it soft in tone or clear? Do you use "ums" and "you knows"? Do you sound authoritative or tentative?

As in the self-analysis section, it's a good idea to jot down your reactions to what you hear. What do you like and what needs improvement?

My Taped Meeting

What I Liked: **What Needs Improvement:**

_____   _____

_____   _____

_____   _____

_____   _____

_____   _____

Video

There's no substitute for videotaping when you want to "see it like it is." Videotaping can be done in an informal, inexpensive way, or by a professional who is coaching you on your presentation style. The quick way to accomplish this is to use your own (or a borrowed) video camera and tape yourself doing a presentation, the opening to a meeting, or even a one-on-one role-play with a friend. Dress in business attire in order to get the best "look" at yourself.

- Was your appearance appropriate and professional, or did you cringe at the way you looked?
- Did your clothing and the colors you wore distinguish you in a positive way, or make you fade into the background?
- Did you use body language and gestures to accentuate your points, or did they distract?
- Was your demeanor pleasant and warm, or did you seem overly serious and dour?
- Did you connect with the audience, or feel that they weren't engaged?
- Were your gestures smooth, or did you have nervous, distracting habits?
- Did you comfortably move around the room, or woodenly stand in one position?

This exercise has opened the eyes of every woman who has experienced it and, in many cases, made an important and positive change in their styles. It is essential to get both the "big picture" of how you look and sound as well as a view of the smaller details that might be a distraction from your presentation.

Don't forget to take notes as you watch your video—several times.

What I Noticed on My Video

What I Liked: **What Needs Improvement:**

_____   _____

_____   _____

_____   _____

_____   _____

_____   _____

Buddy System

Do you have a colleague in the business world or someone else whom you can truly trust—and who will be brutally honest? If the answer is yes, you can enlist the aid of your friend, perhaps volunteering that you will give him or her feedback, too. Depending on your relationship, a "buddy" can be a friend, coworker, or even your manager.

- A buddy can be extremely helpful by role-playing with you before a presentation or meeting. *This can be very useful in sorting out potential problems or issues before they arise in a meeting.*
- A buddy who works with you can help in meetings by signaling if you are falling into a "communication trap" such as rambling, using discounting language, or speaking too softly. *Several women I coached at a very large company made a pact to help and support each other, not only with private feedback and critiques, but in meetings. Whenever they were in meetings together, they had a prearranged way of signaling the others if they were saying something that was detracting from their message.*
- Buddies who are coworkers—or even your manager—can give feedback on a specific situation as well as critiques based on general observations about your communication style in various settings. *Ask your manager for feedback after a meeting: "Did I get my points across?" "Did we accomplish what we needed to?"*

Suggestions from My Buddy:

_____

_____

_____

_____

_____

Becoming a More Powerful Voice

Given the enormity of the communication gap between men and women, sharpening our communication styles is critical to achieving success. It is something women need to continually work on over time. By drawing on our natural strengths as listeners and communicators, and refining those things that don't work well for us in corporate America, women will become more powerful communicators and achieve greater influence with their colleagues.

Through your observations, the results of the quizzes and exercises, and brutal honesty, evaluate yourself as a communicator and take steps to eliminate your problem areas. Since we have established that the bar is set very high for women, even one flaw can be a major detractor. Ask yourself the hard questions, and if you don't like the answers—*do something about it.* It will be a major advantage.

What Is *Your* Communication Style?

Here are several quizzes to determine how you communicate and identify key areas you will want to examine.

Do you stay on message?	Yes	No
1. Do people tell you they don't understand what you're getting at?	☐	☐
2. Has feedback you've received shown you that you are frequently misunderstood?	☐	☐
3. Do you often notice that you've forgotten the point you were trying to make?	☐	☐
4. Do you find yourself rambling when you speak?	☐	☐
5. Do people finish your sentences?	☐	☐

If you have one yes, it sounds like your communication is focused. If you have two or more yeses, you'll want to reassess your speaking style. You may find that you are off target with your message and frequently misunderstood. Start using notes to keep yourself on message, use the power of silence more effectively, and pause to check periodically that you are being understood. These clarifiers, such as "Are you with me?" or "Am I being clear?" will help you stay on course.

Do you maintain your poise at all times?	Yes	No
1. Does your voice change in pitch or tone when you are excited, passionate, or angry?	☐	☐
2. Do you find yourself speaking too quickly?	☐	☐

	Yes	No
3. Do you do a lot of gesturing?	☐	☐
4. Do you pout?	☐	☐
5. Are you emotional at work?	☐	☐
6. Do you show your anger or frustration in your voice?	☐	☐
7. Do you find that people often hit your "hot buttons"?	☐	☐
8. Have people approached you after a meeting asking if you're okay?	☐	☐

If you have fewer than three yeses, you are usually pretty cool. If you have three or more yeses, you're not staying calm and cool when it's important to do so. People may view you as irrational—even unstable—and they may hesitate to discuss sensitive issues with you. Try to determine the cause of your behavior. If it is deep seated in nature, you may want to think about getting professional help. Become aware of the "triggers" that may cause you to get angry and strategically plan ahead how to handle them. This heightened awareness will help you modify and control behavior.

Are you impactful in promoting yourself and your ideas?	Yes	No
1. Have you had your ideas grabbed by someone else?	☐	☐
2. Does your tone sound tentative?	☐	☐
3. Are you afraid to interrupt?	☐	☐
4. Do you ask to speak before speaking?	☐	☐
5. Do you raise your hand to speak in a meeting?	☐	☐
6. Do you hesitate when asked to describe your career strengths?	☐	☐
7. Do you mumble?	☐	☐
8. Do you downplay your successes and accomplishments?	☐	☐

If you've answered yes fewer than three times, you usually promote yourself in meetings. If you have three or more yeses, it's time to work on how you communicate in meetings. Otherwise you will be seen as passive and non-participatory, which can cause you to be sidelined. Start being more assertive—and speak up sooner. Keep a list of your accomplishments handy—and refer to it. Step up to new opportunities for showcasing your skills.

Does your language enhance your image?	Yes	No
1. Do you find yourself using words like "I think," "like," "maybe," "perhaps," and "you know" often?	☐	☐
2. Do you often appear to be asking permission?	☐	☐
3. Do you fill in your silences with "ums" and "ahs"?	☐	☐
4. Do you ever use incorrect grammar or mispronounce words?	☐	☐

If you have fewer than two yeses, you seem to use your language skills well. If you have two or more yeses, get to work on your language skills or risk being viewed as unpolished or unsophisticated. Develop your skills through listening carefully to yourself and others. Ask for feedback on your presentations and consider engaging a speech coach.

These quizzes should bring you closer to understanding your communication style—and where you need to do more work. This type of self-evaluation, and making necessary adjustments, will give you a leg up on most of your colleagues.

Women and Conflict

Conflict is an integral part of workplace communication—and an area that many women would rather avoid. Research shows that men have a more dominant conflict management style, while women often use avoidance as a strategy. Managing conflict situations, however, is an important component of successful leadership.

How do you deal with workplace conflict?	Yes	No
1. Do you feel intimidated and back away from conflict?	☐	☐
2. Do let negative feelings build up inside you until your anger is out of control?	☐	☐
3. Do you often try to accommodate others at any cost?	☐	☐
4. Do you find yourself in the role of "peacemaker" among coworkers?	☐	☐
5. Do you ever get emotional in the face of a conflict?	☐	☐

If you have two or fewer yeses, you seem to have the ability to deal with conflict in a healthy way. If you have three or more yeses, think about your conflict management style and try to develop the resolve and know-how to deal with conflict in an effective and appropriate manner.

Marilyn's colleague had a penchant for office gossip, and it had become his habit to stop in her office and share the news about coworkers. Though his visits had become an unwelcome disturbance, Marilyn took pride in getting along with everyone in the office. She didn't want to risk hurting Rob's feelings by rebuffing what had become intrusive behavior. So she bottled up her annoyance and listened to his stories while keeping one eye on the clock, until one day when she was on a very tight project deadline. When Rob did his "knock-knock" routine and sauntered in, she exploded. "Rob—can't you see I'm in the middle of something?" she yelled. "Stop wasting my time with gossip and just let me do my work for once!" She turned bright red as he backed out of the office.

Since women have been socialized to be "nice," we are prone to letting things fester in the name of courtesy. However, as in Marilyn's case, something relatively small can quickly be blown out of proportion, resulting in hurt feelings and problems between the colleagues for a long time to come.

Tip: Deal with it and move on!

If you are having a problem with a coworker, don't let it irritate you until you get angry. Identify the problem and address it with him or her. By trying to avoid the issue, you may be spending valuable time trying to smooth things over and make them work—instead of facing the conflict and solving it. The latter shows leadership and hopefully won't leave you regretting your actions or words.

When workplace acrimony arises, it is likely that others will observe your handling of the situation, so it is a good time to demonstrate your leadership. Here are a few do's and don'ts to keep in mind.

Do:

- Be direct about a troubling issue
- Label the problem
- Address the situation appropriately
- Deal with it in a timely manner

Don't:

- Continually smooth over problems
- Lose control over your emotions

- Allow things to get personal
- Let a conflict drag on

Solving Disagreements

As we discussed earlier in the chapter, many women are great listeners and empathizers. Therefore, it isn't hard to see why we often get involved in helping others solve their conflicts. We excel at providing a sympathetic ear and support to colleagues who have problems. However, if you frequently find yourself playing the "peacemaker," you may want to reconsider your role. In addition to being a time-consuming task, it is not likely to be valued or appreciated by the management of your organization. In any case, it is worth remembering that you want to be seen as a leader rather than a behind-the-scenes friend to all.

Women can, however, use their inherent traits in a positive way during conflicts. We can channel those important qualities like listening, collaborating, and problem-solving into providing strong leadership in difficult circumstances.

Robin was sitting in the weekly departmental meeting when two of her male colleagues began to disagree over the best way to proceed on a project. As the back-and-forth accelerated and became heated, Robin's first instinct was to shrink into her seat, stay quiet, and see what happened. However, she quickly realized the outcome of their verbal scuffle would directly affect her group's work and she decided to step in. She sat up straight, took a deep breath, and then spoke up to get their attention. Her intervention seemed to calm things down as she clearly summarized the issues and identified the differences she saw. When she finished speaking, the conversation continued with a much calmer tone, and with some give-and-take, the issues were resolved and everyone left on good terms.

By Robin's taking command of the situation, she not only got the result she wanted for her employees, but she also demonstrated her leadership to her peers. She overcame her impulse to avoid the conflict, maintained her composure, and identified the issues at hand. By doing so, she was able to turn down her colleagues' volume and get the meeting back on track.

Pushing Back

In the face of receiving a "no," studies show that women are likely to accept the answer and give in. Men, who are frequently more competitive, are more apt to challenge an unwanted response. Women would rather avoid an argu-ment than pursue the issue and challenge their boss or colleague. They may feel intimidated or simply want to avoid unpleasantness. However, if you always back down and are easily intimidated, you may be seen as weak and, ultimately, not as a leader. Remember, good leadership entails championing positions, standing up for your employees, and negotiating to get what you want. Those who work for you and with you are counting on that!

Jaye headed into her boss's office for an annual meeting she dreaded. She needed to get approval for her department's budget. She clearly remem-bered that at the previous year's meeting, things had gotten chilly. Her boss had immediately declared that her numbers were way out of line—and the meeting had gone downhill from there. Later, she heard her colleague brag-ging that he stood up to the boss and got his budget approved. Today, Jaye had backup in her pocket and was determined to be forceful in defending her proposal. As Jaye and Mark began the meeting, Mark quickly dismissed the numbers as "too high" and looked annoyed. Last year Jaye had caved in—she was not going to do it again. She steeled herself, brought out her material, and cited the reasons she needed the funds. He pushed back again by saying, "I have people at the top to answer to on this budget!" But she wasn't giving in—and again summarized her position. Mark stayed quiet for a moment, thinking, and then said he would present what she had recom-mended.

Jaye had learned from experience, and she was more prepared for her annual budget meeting this time around. She wasn't going to take "no" for an answer without doing all she could to persuade her boss. In this situa-tion, Jaye earned respect from Mark by not taking his first "no" as a final answer. She had solid facts on her side, was strong in her conviction, and ended up the better for it.

Emotions

Many women have a tendency to get emotional when they are stressed, angry, or excited. This may cause them to get teary, their voice to tremble, or their body to shake. These manifestations present a dilemma when in the workplace since men often feel uncomfortable and may even get annoyed when this occurs. Men aren't sure how to handle the situation because they don't understand it and may even see it as manipulative. If you are a person who reacts this way when conflict occurs, there are a few things to think about.

- Understand what triggers your emotion
- Strategize ahead of time about how to calm yourself
- Anticipate possible situations in advance

If you have taken these steps and still find yourself reacting emotionally—explain yourself. Own it by saying something like, "While it may appear I'm overreacting, it's part of my DNA to get excited and emotional about things. Please bear with me." By putting it out there, the situation is defused, and you should have the pause you need to pull yourself together. Investing time in changing how you respond in conflict situations will not only help you feel better about yourself—but it will improve relationships with colleagues.

Conflict is never easy, but by thinking about your own patterns of behavior and ways to handle problem situations, you will have more confidence in the future when there is discord in the office.

CHAPTER 2

Make the Connection

Network Strategically to Advance Your Career

N ETWORKING WORKS. There's no denying it. Years ago, Michele was at a fund-raising event and met a woman who was very interested in transferring her skills as executive director for a nonprofit organization into the for-profit world. Michele liked her and offered to help develop her marketability for the business world even though she was already very busy. The two met a couple of times at Michele's office to critique the woman's résumé, and review her options and strategy as she embarked on her campaign to transition to a new role. Time passed—and several years later, at another event, this same woman, whom Michele had long ago lost track of, approached her and said, "Do you remember me? You really helped me a few years ago when I most needed it. Well, guess what? I'm now at Procter & Gamble and have achieved a senior position there." She went on to tell Michele that she had a large project she thought Michele's firm could help her with and they set up a time to meet. Michele was both surprised and delighted to unexpectedly receive a $2 million piece of business from her! Networking *can* produce rewards when you least expect them. *It's simple logic—do right by people and they'll eventually do right by you.*

42

Business gets done through relationships. When women feel excluded and cut off from information in the corporate culture, it is often due to their resistance to relationship building at work, because women, more so than men, have been programmed to spend their limited time doing their work well instead of doing what it takes to develop strategic relationships. In a research survey conducted by The Leader's Edge, senior men and women were asked, "How important was networking in reaching your current position?" The men rated it as far more important than the women did, indicating that they place a higher value on networking and may more clearly understand its benefits.

How do *your* networking skills rate? Take the following quiz and see.

How do your networking skills rate?	Yes	No
1. Do you believe networking has value for you personally?	☐	☐
2. Do you believe networking has value for your business?	☐	☐
3. Are you enthusiastic about networking opportunities?	☐	☐
4. Do you have networking goals (i.e., meeting targets)?	☐	☐
5. Do you have at least one networking meeting a week?	☐	☐
6. Are at least half of your meetings face-to-face?	☐	☐
7. Are you networking with colleagues outside of your functional area?	☐	☐
8. Are you networking with colleagues outside of your company?	☐	☐
9. Are you networking with thought leaders, experts, and competitors?	☐	☐
10. Do you network with people who are not close friends or coworkers?	☐	☐
11. Do you spend time and network with people with whom you sometimes have tension or difficulty?	☐	☐
12. Do you give as much information and assistance in your networking as you take?	☐	☐

If you answered yes to six or more questions, it sounds like you are doing some valuable networking to broaden your visibility. Keep up with what you are doing and look for even more ways to network strategically. If you didn't get six yeses, you need to develop a better appreciation of the benefits of networking and have some serious work to do on your networking skills.

The Importance of Strategic Networking

There are two key components in making strategic connections with contacts who are important to your future—and our research and experience show that women are losing out in both categories. The first is building relationships *within* your company. These alliances with colleagues, bosses, clients, consultants, and vendors are vital and provide the foundation for your future within your organization.

Ashley, a corporate attorney, excitedly called to tell her former boss and mentor about a major promotion she had received. The vice president title Ashley had achieved had been a long-term goal, and she admitted that she had always thought she would be judged for this promotion solely on the quality of her legal work. She now saw that she had been a bit naïve and that getting to know the people in her company who were influential in the decision—the president, her boss's boss, and the head of human resources—was crucial to her success. The effort she had put into building these relationships by showing her interest in the company, talking about her projects, and making them comfortable with her both as a colleague and an individual had been a key element in the decision to promote her. Though she knew they had always valued her as a contributor, they needed to see her as a leader and a team player in order to seriously consider her for this promotion.

The second "connection" category is strategic networking *outside* of your company. Strategic networking can provide many benefits to you in your present position as well as in future positions. Many people think that networking is synonymous with looking for a job and, considering that more than 80 percent of executive positions are found through networking, clearly it works. It may well be that contacts will lead you to a job opportunity now or in the future. There are, however, many other possible rewards in making contacts, including:

- Gaining valuable information
- Becoming well-known and well-liked
- Learning interpersonal and leadership skills
- Building allies and developing reciprocal business relationships
- Brainstorming ideas/solving problems
- Acquiring new business opportunities and leads
- Understanding various outside organizations
- Assessing your worth
- Discovering a community or professional group

- Being asked to join a board or committee position
- Helping others

Be honest—did you really think networking could benefit you in so many ways? While strategic networking and relationship building require an additional time commitment during the workday and outside of work, the benefits in terms of one's personal, business, and career satisfaction are undeniable.

Andrea was a financial sales executive who spent the day at her computer and on the phone in her office in order to get the maximum amount of work done. She didn't pay attention to the fact that the water cooler just down the hall was an informal gathering place for her colleagues. In fact, she dismissed their conversations as a waste of time. But the truth is that, by not joining in these informal sessions, she missed out on getting to know her peers, leads for new business, and ideas that would help her. The men were uneasy with her—they felt they didn't know her since she wasn't part of their casual conversations. Eventually, she came to understand that the conversations were actually a valuable resource, and she began to join her peers at lunch and "water cooler" discussions. This led to developing better relationships with her colleagues and collaborating with them on business initiatives. In addition, through hearing their stories, she picked up several creative new tactics for developing business. She realized that these relationships were at least as productive—if not more so—as the quantity and quality of her work.

Tip: Networking Is a Contact Sport

Don't wait for information to come to you. Get out of your office, join a conversation, and get in on the informal network "action." You never know what you'll learn. You just might find out who's on the way up (or down), the scoop on how your colleague landed a new account, or why an impromptu meeting has been scheduled. To feel included as part of the team, share some nonconfidential information of your own from time to time.

Identify Your Key Professional Contacts

The first step in the networking process is identifying and analyzing your *key professional contacts: those people who have a stake, personally and/or professionally, in your success or failure in your organization.* They could be a boss, peer, direct report, colleague—or even a client or vendor.

Ann is a senior vice president in charge of a significant product portfolio for an international consumer goods company. Kate, who also holds the SVP title but is ranked slightly higher, is in an entirely different division of the organization. Kate's position requires that she regularly attend global meetings at which Ann's product line—and her name—often are mentioned. Kate is therefore, *indirectly,* a stakeholder in Ann's success.

If Kate doesn't know Ann, she cannot comment on her work, instead saying something like, "I really don't know what Ann is doing on that project." If she's had a negative experience or encounter with Ann, she might downplay her work by saying, "I really don't think you can count on Ann." On the other hand, if she knows Ann and is invested in her success, she is more likely to say, "I just spoke to Ann about that the other day—and she's got some very interesting ideas in the pipeline." Or, "Ann would be perfect to take the lead on that project and I would like to help her." *One positive statement or nod by a key contact can "make you"—just as a blank look or dismissive sentence can "break you."*

It is important to Ann's success that she considers Kate as one of her key contacts and reaches out to her periodically. And, it would benefit Ann to do some research and learn what she can about Kate's style, interests, and issues. This can be accomplished by observing who Kate's colleagues are and finding an opportunity to ask some open-ended questions. This way, she will have some background when she meets with Kate, so it will be easier to get to know her and make Kate feel comfortable with her and her work.

In the next exercise, you'll think through and define the people within your professional circle who should be important to *you,* and the relationship you currently have with them. Once you develop this list, you will have a better idea of the steps you need to take to expand and maintain your relationships.

Complete the following analysis and be creative in thinking about your key professional contacts. Ask yourself: Who needs to know me? Who should understand what I'm trying to achieve in my work? Who needs to be aware of my experience, skills, and abilities? What relationship would I like to have with the people listed, and what do I need to do to make it happen? The first chart has some examples. The second chart is for you to complete.

The next story is a good illustration of the importance of "people development" to your success in your job. Diana had to work hard to overcome her separation from friends and colleagues when she moved to the United States from England to become vice president of an international medical

Analysis of My Key Professional Contacts (example)

Category	Name	Current Relationship/ Status	Stake in Success	Relationship Desired	Next Steps
Superior(s)	Joe Jones	Boss's boss. No informal contact, only see at biweekly meetings.	Very influential— key player in future promotions.	More comfortable level of inter- action, more casual and regular.	Stop in office once a week to update him, find out about his interests beyond work; send e-mails or articles on pertinent topics.
Peer(s)	Kate Reilly	She runs a division that interfaces with my group. Don't know her well.	Highly regarded, her opinion of me is important.	More regular contact and exchange of ideas/info.	Call to ask her to lunch.
Direct Report(s)	Roy Barbour	Was in my department when I took over. We get along well.	Went to school with Joe Jones's son, often talks to Joe.	Positive boss/ employee relationship.	Make a point to informally "status" with him every so often.

Continued

Analysis of **My Key Professional Contacts (example) (Continued)**

Category	Name	Current Relationship/ Status	Stake in Success	Relationship Desired	Next Steps
Client(s)	Cara Morgan	I participate in client meetings with her. Know her only formally.	She is an important client and very vocal, so her opinion of me counts.	Warmer, more casual interaction.	Go to client meetings earlier to have informal conversations with her.
Vendor(s)	Lanny Whitehouse	He's been a vendor with the company for twenty years and we schmooze.	Has lunch with Joe regularly, has the opportunity to say something positive about me.	Continue being friendly in a professional way.	Notice when he comes in and speak with him.
Consultant(s)	Marnie Lerner	Is considered a "whiz kid" by management. Not sure she likes me.	Management highly values her recommendations and opinions so better make sure she thinks well of me.	Get to know her better and create a positive relationship.	Find a way to talk with her more informally and let her know my work.

Analysis of My Key Professional Contacts

Category	Name	Current Relationship/ Status	Stake in Success	Relationship Desired	Next Steps
Superior(s)					
Peer(s)					
Direct Report(s)					
Client(s)					
Vendor(s)					
Consultant(s)					

organization. She had dual networking challenges: getting her family settled and integrating into a new job position. Her children's schools and her neighbors provided a nice group of people outside of work, which helped make her family feel welcome. Happily, things seemed to come together on that score. At work, she had to resist her inclination to concentrate on her job and the people in her department and instead, go out and meet her peers and colleagues. In reality, new leaders have a window of only three to four months in which to establish their credibility. So, she immediately made a list of all the people she identified as key to her success.

After making her list, she circled back to her boss to let him know her networking plan and time line, making sure she had his support. She worked hard to create and build a strong support infrastructure within her company, and very quickly was able to establish her presence and credibility. She was truly building her foundation for the future, touching base with people, getting crucial information, and establishing ongoing lines of communication. She was happy with the results she achieved—in record time—and knew that it would be invaluable to her success in her future career as a leader.

Identifying Your Broad Network

Since you've now identified your "work-related" network, let's add to your base by making a list of your broader networking contacts. This will help you begin to understand where you have strong networking potential. Over years of outplacement counseling, I've seen many examples of people who are experts in their areas and have achieved high levels at their companies, but who have spent virtually no time pursuing outside activities. When they lost their jobs, they were suddenly in urgent need of contacts and visibility in the community. In spite of their years of work experience, they had to start at square one in terms of developing contacts. Most of these executives regretted their lack of participation in outside networking activities and they were determined not to let it happen again.

Remember, *everyone* is a potential contact in the context of broad networking, including:

Friends
Relatives
Neighbors
Professional acquaintances

Colleagues
Former colleagues
School buddies (alumni from college, high school, or graduate school)
Professional advisors (lawyer, accountants)
Acquaintances through religious affiliation
Others (be creative—do you play a team sport or belong to a gym? Are
    your children in a playgroup?)

To help you get started, list each name within the appropriate category, along with their position and your current relationship with them. Put in the frequency of your interaction with that person and any special information you have about his or her interests. Again, we've given you a sample network chart to give you some ideas. Think hard as you develop your list, and you might be surprised at the number of contacts you already have.

Once you've made a list of your broader network of contacts and divided it into categories, look carefully at your list, and ask yourself the following questions:

- Do you have contacts in a variety of areas or does most of your network fall under one or two categories?
- Do you notice gaps that you'd like to fill?
- How often are you in touch with the people you've listed?
- Is your network open and diverse?

Ideal strategic networks are "open," meaning they have many contacts outside your functional area and company, and "diverse" in that they put you in contact with people who are not close friends, coworkers, or just like you professionally, ethnically, and gender-wise. This more free-flowing network can result in much more opportunity than a *"closed"* network, which has less diversity and fewer, more intense contacts located entirely within your department, company, or safety zone.

Consider diversity from several additional standpoints such as age, status, country, and education. Does your network touch different types of people from different professions and levels of authority? In a truly open and global network, contacts extend outside your organization to thought leaders, competitors, gurus, and peers worldwide in your industry. If you only know people in your profession at the same level as you are, you will limit yourself. The more diverse your network is, the more opportunities you can create.

Analysis of My Broad Network (example)

Category	Name	Position	Current Relationship	Frequency of Contact	Special Interests
Friends	Jane Smith	Consulting firm partner	Members of same book club	About nine times a year	She likes to read nonfiction books
Relatives	Lonnie Small	COO of a manufacturing business	Brother-in-law	Twice a month	My nephew—his son!
Neighbors	Donald White	Sales manager for competitor	Lives two doors down from me	Every week or so	Has a dog same breed as mine
Former Work Colleagues	Lucy Mifflin	Sales	Members of the same professional organization	Every month	She's a workaholic and could use a break
School Buddies	BJ Skinner	Architect	See every summer	Several times a year	Alumni club officer for my college

Analysis of My Broad Network (example) (Continued)

Category	Name	Position	Current Relationship	Frequency of Contact	Special Interests
Professional Advisors (CPAs, MDs, lawyers)	Kim Matlack	Prominent surgeon at major hospital	Did my son's operation	See occasionally around town	Plays tennis
Acquaintance through Religious Affiliation	Tim Boyle	Attorney at insurance co.	Know through church	See every so often	Sings in church choir

Analysis of My Broad Network

Category	Name	Position	Current Relationship	Frequency of Contact	Special Interests
Friends					
Relatives					
Neighbors					
Former Work Colleagues					
School Buddies					
Professional Advisors (CPAs, MDs, lawyers)					
Acquaintance through Religious Affiliation					

Think about *your* network and answer the following questions:

Does everyone in your network know everyone else? If your network is made up of people who all know each other, you may find you get a lot of recycled information instead of new ideas and creativity. By being aware of where you do and do not have contacts, you can begin to create strategies for meeting and developing relationships with more and varied people.

To what extent is your network contributing to your business and career objectives? What areas should you concentrate on to make your network more diverse and productive? Which categories need more contacts? What type of contacts would be most beneficial in terms of your business and career goals?

What actions can you take to build your network? Perhaps there are specific events you can attend (college reunions? professional or civic associations? meetings? seminars?) to build relationships. Or, maybe you already know people whom you haven't viewed as potential contacts. Those relationships can be cultivated.

Adding to Your Network

To move to a more "open" network of contacts, make a list of people you haven't considered before who are outside your current network and whom you should—or would—like to know. Consider people inside and outside your organization. Think about colleagues across your organization, not just in your division, and those you haven't paid attention to recently. Expand your list with contacts you have met at seminars and conferences, and people you know in your community. Reassess the value of knowing them better.

List people you'd like to add to your network and the steps you will take to further the relationship. The first chart gives you some examples. Use the second chart to list the people *you* should get to know better.

How Networking Works

Networking should, when executed correctly, be something that makes all parties feel good. People like to refer business or make introductions for others because most people like to be helpful.

Ellen was hired not long ago by the publisher of a well-known regional magazine for a prominent senior position. She had just relocated from another part of the country where she had a similar position with a smaller publication. She was excited about her new position as editor-in-chief, but

My Expanded Network (example)

Category	Name/Current Relationship	Value of Expanded Relationship	Next Step
Peers	Ellen Bard in accounting. Don't know her.	She's active in community organizations and can help me connect.	Call her to set up an introductory meeting.
Superiors	Jean Smith, head of Operations	Since she heads a different area of the company, I can learn from her.	Find someone we both know and set up a lunch.
Competition	Bob Bartlett at S&G Company. Met at professional meeting.	On the board of the United Way. Can help me get on one of their committees.	Phone him for lunch.
Community Leaders	Sandy Hill, head of Pets for Life	She knows almost everyone!	Go to her next fund-raiser.
Political Leaders	Melissa Caro, my state representative	She's well connected. May be able to give me advice on industry legislation.	Write to her to introduce myself and the company.

My Expanded Network

Category	Name/Current Relationship	Value of Expanded Relationship	Next Step
Peers			
Superiors			
Competition			
Community Leaders			
Political Leaders			

You now have a start on developing a more open network.

she had recently moved to Philadelphia after living and working in the South since college, so she had few contacts. In her position, she was expected to understand the region's business community, be aware of the issues, and know the significant players. She had to get up to speed quickly in order to make an impact in her job.

What she needed was a network of connected business leaders to help her integrate into the city and the region. She decided a good place to start was with high-level women, and with the help of her publisher, she worked to develop a list of eight women business leaders, all of whom were on boards and committees throughout the region. They set up a "power lunch" and invited the women to meet her. They all accepted and the lunch was a success. The group welcomed her and everyone was eager to support and assist her. They shared their insights about important issues, and offered to include her in upcoming meetings, make introductions to other key players (men *and* women), and invite her to join key organizations. They were delighted to be able to help her make business connections and become better known, and had no doubt that she would be willing and able to help *them* in the future. The result was that through this "instant network" she was able to get a jump start in her new position, which is just as important as learning the job.

Tip: Give and You Shall Receive

You don't have to be looking for something yourself to profit from networking. Approach each interaction or introduction with the thought, "How can I help this person?" and you will make a strong and important connection each time. When you meet new contacts, ask yourself: Is there an introduction that would help them? A contact in a particular industry they would be interested in? An organization they might like to join? If you view contacts from this point of view, you'll find that when you have a need, there will be many people willing and able to help you!

Take Your Network to a Higher Power

Networking involves not only making connections in order to expand influence and build relationships, but deepening and broadening the quality of your network.

This quiz will help you evaluate whether you are effectively building *your* network.

Are you building your network?	Yes	No
1. Do you stay in regular communication with contacts?	☐	☐
2. Do you make new connections through introductions?	☐	☐
3. Are you receptive to introductions and requests for meetings?	☐	☐
4. Do you participate in informal gatherings of work colleagues?	☐	☐
5. Do you host networking events and meetings?	☐	☐
6. Do you act as a "connector" to bring together company departments and functional areas?	☐	☐
7. Do you act as a "connector" to bring together people outside your organization?	☐	☐
8. Do you connect with your network using all the available communication tools (meetings, e-mails, voice mail, etc.)?	☐	☐

If you answered yes to five or more questions, you're taking important steps to build your network. Continue looking for connections. If you have too many nos, you need to concentrate on the value of connecting with others.

Get Involved in Outside Activities

If you look at the résumés of the leaders in industry, you will see that many of the most effective and successful people in business understand that volunteer work is an integral part of networking and adds to their leadership experience and development.

There are many reasons why women should consider getting involved in a community organization or extracurricular activity. It is important to be an advocate, help others, make your voice heard, and contribute. In addition, it makes excellent business sense.

Remember, while you are giving time to a social cause, charity, or professional association, you're helping your career by gaining leadership experience, networking opportunities, and business contacts.

In order to gauge the level of your activity outside of your job, and whether it is adequate, complete the following survey. Take this quiz and find out!

Are you involved enough in outside activities?	*Yes*	*No*
1. Do you use your skills and experience to help community and civic organizations?	☐	☐
2. Do you sit on any boards of outside organizations?	☐	☐
3. Have you carved out time outside of work to volunteer?	☐	☐
4. Are you a working member of a professional, civic, or charitable organization?	☐	☐
5. Do you consider volunteer work to be a strategic part of your career and leadership development?	☐	☐
6. Do you have an active network of contacts outside of your business and personal friends?	☐	☐
7. Do you engage in any extracurricular activities that build contacts?	☐	☐
8. Are you receptive when asked to participate in outside civic and community activities?	☐	☐
9. Do you make time for outside activities that are important to your job?	☐	☐
10. Do you make it known that you are available to participate in outside activities or join boards?	☐	☐

If you've answered yes to more than six of the above questions, you're on the right track for becoming more involved in activities outside of work and raising your profile in the community. Four to six yeses? Though you have some things going, you may want to step up your activities. Fewer than four yes answers—you are not taking advantage of the learning opportunities provided in outside civic and community work. You may find yourself left behind if you don't change your viewpoint.

In essence, while you *give* experience that is extremely valuable to community organizations, you also *gain* the opportunity to enhance and build skills that will be beneficial to you. If you are having trouble seeing how you could add value, the following are some examples of this.

What You Can Offer a Community Organization

- Marketing and PR advice and input for events, fund-raising
- Management and personnel guidance
- Financial expertise on how to save costs and leverage dollars
- Technical help in how to manage database client and donor information
- Contacts for resources and donations
- Leadership experience for driving initiatives

What You Can Gain by Becoming Involved

- Exposure and visibility through chairing or hosting events and public speaking
- Persuasion and influence skills developed through fund-raising
- Team-building skills through leading projects and initiatives
- Networking skills honed by making introductions for the organization

As a partner and COO of a consulting firm, Melanie now firmly believes that her work in community organizations has changed her business life. Earlier, she hadn't thought of community organizations as vital to her business, and was caught up in growing her company, making the numbers work, and building the business. All of a sudden, she and her CEO, who also spent most of his time in the office, realized that the business had reached a critical stage of growth and they needed to explore options for their company. There were lots of questions on the radar screen, and she and her boss had limited contacts to help with answers. They just didn't have many connections with executives who might have experience to share regarding a merger, acquisition, and other options, nor were they or their company well known in the community.

Melanie jump-started her effort to develop a higher profile by going to professional meetings, identifying peers in similar service businesses, and asking people to breakfast and lunch. Each contact led to another, and she slowly grew a network of people with whom she shared ideas and gained information. She learned whole new ways of doing business *and* gave her and her company the visibility they needed. Ultimately, a contact put them in touch with a larger firm interested in expanding its services, and Melanie's company was acquired.

Tip: Create a Win-Win-Win

Introduce two people in your network and everyone wins. The person who gives a referral (you!) feels powerful and connected. The individual on the receiving end is grateful because his or her problem is potentially resolved. And, the person being referred to is delighted to meet a new contact or perhaps get new business. It's a win-win-win. Everyone in the transaction is pleased.

Choose What's Right for You

Getting involved with a cause about which you feel passionate is personally satisfying *and* integral to leadership development. By playing a key role in

your community you can observe other leaders' styles, thinking, and problem solving. You'll meet people with whom you share common interests and
ideals, which can be the basis of a real bond. The people who work together
in a community effort are likely to genuinely enjoy each other and want to
do business together. Find what it is you care about and the business will
follow.

Sometimes people are clear about what causes they want to support. But
many people have trouble figuring out where to begin. The following set of
questions should help direct you to specific activities and organizations that
might be of interest. Fill in the answers in areas that apply to you.

Where Do Your Interests Lie?

Do you have a hobby that could translate into an organization or
cause?

Do you have a friend or relative who has struggled with a physical or
mental condition? Could this translate into an organization or cause?

Is there a cultural activity that you particularly enjoy? Could this activity translate into an organization or cause?

Are you interested in current affairs and politics? Could this interest
translate into an organization or cause?

Are people you admire involved in a particular activity or organization?

Have you attended an organization event that you enjoyed?

Is there an activity or organization from which you believe you could
learn and develop new skills?

Do you have a favorite cause to which you donate money?

Is there a prestigious organization in your community that you aspire
to join?

Your objective is to uncover those activities that would be most rewarding for you. If your sister is fighting an illness, that cause can be a labor of love. If you always dreamed of being a musician, joining an orchestra committee may be just right. Maybe you are crazy about your city or town since moving there two years ago—in that case, the chamber of commerce or visitors' center may be your calling.

If you are still unsure, here's another way to identify a cause that will interest you. Do any of the following categories trigger your interest? Put a checkmark next to the ones you want to consider.

My Interests

☐ Culture and the arts (e.g., orchestra, dance, museums, etc.)

☐ Health and humanities (e.g., United Way, American Heart Association, March of Dimes, etc.)

☐ Community and economic development (e.g., a venture-capital group, industrial development corporation, World Affairs Council, etc.)

☐ Local/regional business (e.g., chamber of commerce, marketing and tourism center, Rotary Club, etc.)

☐ Civic and public affairs (e.g., political parties and/or candidates, school boards, township associations)

☐ Professional and industry (e.g., American Bankers Association, American Bar Association, etc.)

☐ Women (e.g., National Association of Female Executives, The White House Project, local women's groups)

☐ School alumni (e.g., college and university clubs)

Once you've started to narrow down the areas you're interested in, you'll need to find specific organizations in your region. Get a directory of organizations or do an online search. When you have the name of an organization, call and ask for information to be sent to you, and at the same time, ask among friends and work colleagues to see who might be familiar with it or another like it. Chances are, once you have the name of an organization, you can find someone you know who is already involved, or can get an introduction to someone who is.

Does your company have an activity it supports? Perhaps your company supports a specific cause or organization. If your company is engaged in a cause that interests you, get involved.

Does your company have an employee designated to help with community involvement? Many companies have someone whose job it is to link employees to community activities. They may be in community affairs, public relations, or human resources, and they can be very helpful in facilitating introductions, and giving you insights and information.

Are any of your colleagues involved in worthwhile causes? Even if your company isn't strongly connected to a particular cause or activity, you'll probably find colleagues who are involved in a variety of community activities and can give you information.

Tip: Be an Enthusiastic Ambassador

When you serve on a committee or board of an organization, you become a representative for the group. When attending an organization event or activity, consider yourself one of the hosts and make yourself accessible. Introduce yourself to those you don't know, be prepared to answer questions about the organization, and be enthusiastic about the cause. Stimulating interest in your organization is an important part of your committee or board position.

Staying in Touch with Contacts

Once you've accumulated contacts from a broad range of activities, and listed and categorized each individual, you need a solid system to keep you up to date with your follow-ups. You'll want to organize your efforts in a database that allows you to track dates of interactions, keep a file for notes and information, and jog your memory on follow-up.

The format for keeping notes, shown on the next page, captures your contact interactions, complete with details of the meeting or call, and the next steps in your strategy—it even reminds you who referred you to your contact. You can set this up on your computer using a spreadsheet. Update it regularly! Fill out *your* contacts on the second form.

My Contact Notes (example)

Name	Title	Date of Contact	Referral Source	Contact Summary	Future Strategy	Referred To
Sue Stanton	Starlight Bank, One Liberty Sq., Baltimore, MD Phone: 302-233-3300 E-mail Stanton@ Starlight.com	3/15/04	*Jack Bauer,* EVP	Good meeting at her office about possible speaking opps, is Pres. of Bankers Assoc. (Same birthday as mine!)	Call in May to discuss program for future meeting	*Matt Daimler,* another possible speaker
Matt Daimler	Lorien Company, 4400 Oreland Blvd., Towson, MD Phone: 302-876-5000 x11	3/30/04	*Sue Stanton*	Phone call, left message	Try again in 3 days	

My Contact Notes

Name	Title	Date of Contact	Referral Source	Contact Summary	Future Strategy	Referred To

How to Capitalize on Your Network

As you set up your own system, grade your contacts as As, Bs or Cs:

- An "A" person is very important and influential and perhaps a bit intimidating.
- A "B" person has moderate influence and may or may not be a great contact.
- A "C" person has little obvious influence—he or she could be a friend, direct report, or a new contact.

To get started, try your networking skills on your C list. They may surprise you with their insights and advice, and you have less to lose. Get comfortable with your introduction and description of your skills and accomplishments—and then move higher up on your list to the Bs and As. Developing a strategy for each interaction will help you make the best possible impression and maximize your contact.

The steps you take, what you say, and how you say it is critical. Here are some creative ways to connect:

- Set up a formal meeting to discuss a topic of mutual interest.
- Invite an influential contact to attend an event at which you are a speaker or panelist.
- Help contacts stay current by sending them an article or other piece of information they may find of value.
- Plan to attend a meeting or event if you know a senior player will be present. If necessary, use a contact to get invited.

Once you understand your contact's needs, you'll easily be able to find ways to follow up with him or her. It's a great way to forge a relationship based on something that is substantial and a reason to stay in touch. So, while you're talking with someone, listen carefully and try to uncover the need. Then, once it becomes part of the discussion, you have the opening to say, "Let me think about that and get back to you with some ideas . . ." and leave it at that. Now you have a great way to follow up.

Recently Rebecca was at an event and started talking with the president of a local printing company who mentioned that she'd like to become more involved in community organizations. Rebecca asked her a few specific questions about her interests and availability. She told her that she thought she might be able to assist her, wanted to give it some thought, and would contact her soon. A couple of days later, after making some inquiries, Rebecca was able to call and give her the name of the board chairman of a large organization who was very interested in talking with her about a committee position.

How to Make Your Meetings Smooth

In a networking meeting, you'll want to use the first few minutes to take any pressure off your contact and put him or her in a comfort zone. Remember to:

- Be clear about your purpose for the meeting, who referred you, and how much time you'll need. It helps to emphasize that you are looking for information and advice—not a job.
- Do some background investigative work on your contact to find mutual connections and interests.
- Find out about the contact's personality and understand what type of person to expect.
- Rehearse your presentation and prepare questions in advance.
- Set realistic goals for the meeting.

Taking these steps will help prepare you for the conversation.

Tip: Making Contact

When setting up a meeting, use the name of the person who referred you and state the reason for the meeting. Better yet, have your mutual acquaintance e-mail or phone ahead to say you'll be in contact. If no one has referred you, it's more difficult to make contact with an important person—but not impossible. When you phone him or her, identify who you are and say, "I'd like a few minutes of your time to discuss . . ." or "I'm interested in XYZ Organization and since you're on the board, I'd like to get your perspective . . ." or "I heard you speak at a recent meeting and would like your advice on . . ." Be creative!

Put your contacts at ease while giving them a brief summary of your background and reason for the meeting. Pay attention to your personality type, which has an impact on style and delivery. If you are more on the introverted side, you'll want to give special attention to rehearsing introductions and preparing questions in advance. If you are an extrovert, it is especially important to focus and be strategic in your interactions so you don't dominate the conversation. Write down what you plan to say.

Example: The Two-Minute Capsule

Introductory Statement/Name of Referrer/Purpose. Great to meet you, Bob. I'm Diane Groton and my colleague Rich Bowman speaks highly of you. When he told me of your position on the marketing council, I was very interested in meeting you and brainstorming a little.

Summary of Your Background/Accomplishments (for more, see chapter 9). Let me give you a quick snapshot of my background, Bob. I'm director of marketing at the Linder Company—in fact, I've been with them for ten years. There I've helped increase sales revenues by 10 percent without increasing the number of marketing people, and have become a senior officer of the company. Before that, I did graduate work at Penn after several years as a successful sales manager for an investment firm. I wanted to talk with you about a forum for our national marketing people that I'm heading up.

Purpose/Substance of Meeting. I understand that your marketing council recently sponsored a research study and I wanted to explore the possibility of presenting it to my forum, perhaps with a panel of experts.

Tip: Your Time Is Up!

Now, practice your listening skills, take notes, and formulate your questions. This information will go into your database under Contact Summary, and will be a road map for your future interactions and relationship with this individual.

Conclusion and Follow-Up. Before we conclude, is there anyone else you'd recommend I touch base with? Thank you for some great ideas. I truly enjoyed our meeting and will follow up next month. In the meantime, if there's any way I can be of assistance to you, I hope you'll contact me. Again, thank you for your time today.

Remember: End the meeting on time.

Now, try it for an upcoming meeting of your own with one of your identified contacts.

Two-Minute Capsule

Introduction:

Background/Accomplishments:

Purpose/Substance of Meeting:

Conclusion and Follow-Up:

Tip: Close the Loop!

Never let more than four to six weeks go by before reconnecting with someone you've met. This is when the impression you made will begin to fade and you need to loop back through an e-mail, phone call, or letter, and let your contact know that you're working on whatever the two of you talked about. If your contact has provided you with a referral to another person, always let him or her know when you have actually gotten in touch with the person. Keep that psychological investment going!

Women and Networking

Maintaining, growing, and nurturing your network takes time—a commodity which most of us find in short supply. Even so, in order to give yourself the best chance for success, it has to stay on top of your priority list. Accept it as an integral part of your work that will benefit you in your job and your company. As you come to view it as a dynamic and rewarding process, you will want to invest time in it whenever you can.

The unique communication style of women can be a strong asset in networking. One rainy Saturday two mothers, Ann and Sue, sat watching their sons play soccer and started talking. It happened that Ann was one of the top women at a large international company. As their conversation continued, Sue sensed Ann's unease as she talked about her job. Sue took the opportunity to tell Ann she was a career counselor and offered her services if she ever had a need. Ann called Sue soon after they met, and it turned out she was having a career crisis which Sue helped guide her through. Years later, Ann called to tell Sue that she had referred her for an important assignment with another company.

Women are known to have good listening skills and be empathetic, which enables them to forge strong bonds with others and helps build contacts. While these strengths are plusses, like many women, you may have challenges in other areas, such as a lack of assertiveness, difficulty in promoting yourself, and getting bogged down in social chitchat.

In dealing with these issues, here are several techniques to keep in mind:

- Present yourself with presence and style: a polished appearance will help you feel confident and self-assured.
- Use powerful, effective language: a crisp delivery will boost your poise and authority.
- Communicate as a professional: a professional image is critical, especially in initial interactions.
- Keep your eye on the goal: always focus on who you're talking with, how they can help you, and vice versa.

Don't underestimate the value of networking. Capitalize on your innate strengths as a woman, consider the reciprocal value of networking, and carve out the time to become more visible. If women don't invest more time in this activity and give it a high priority on our list of things to do, we will not move as fast as the men.

3

Sell Your Strengths
Distinguish Yourself through Self-Promotion

DONNA ATTENDS a monthly meeting that includes all of the vice presidents who report to the head of her division. During one meeting, their boss, Roy, mentions a new initiative that the executive committee is very interested in moving forward. As he discusses the initiative, it's clear that it's going to be an exciting, high-profile project with maximum exposure and promotion possibilities. Donna starts thinking fast about her experience and skills, how they compare with those of her peers, and whether they fit with the project. As Roy continues talking, she's mentally ticking off the pluses and minuses she can offer this major initiative. She has a track record for some parts of the project, but for others she's not so sure. Maybe she can handle it, though she would need support in a couple of areas that she's not totally familiar with. Maybe she should think about it a little more . . . maybe . . .

Just at that moment, her colleague Jim clears his throat and addresses the boss. "Roy, this project is right up my alley. I've successfully handled the Widener project and we practically doubled our productivity in my most recent assignment. I can do a great job on this one for you—give it to me and I can start right away." Everyone in the meeting views Jim as a hero and he is awarded the project while Donna has just let this opportunity slip away. While she was deciding whether she was qualified to head up the project, Jim jumped in and grabbed it.

This, unfortunately, is an all too common illustration of the contrasting styles of men and women in promoting themselves in the workplace.

Men are more comfortable in promoting their strengths and accomplishments than women, and are greater risk-takers. They understand the importance of self-promotion and use it effectively to gain money and power, while the women executives we interviewed consistently identified it as something that does not come naturally. Instead, many women have the misguided belief that they can rely on fairness and recognition, believing that, "If I work hard and do my job well, people will notice." So, while men are out promoting themselves by talking about their talents and abilities, many women simply reject the concept as bragging. They don't see it as something that is directly related to their success. As one savvy senior vice president in investment banking advised, "Females need to toot their own horns more. Don't wait to be asked about what you're doing. Instead, let people in the organization know about your accomplishments. The chairman of our company said of all the e-mails and voice mail messages he gets from employees about deals they closed, problems they solved—99 percent of them are from men!"

In fact, more than 60 percent of the women surveyed by The Leader's Edge said that men are better at promoting themselves. This may be a result of the fact that more than half of those same women felt that women are less confident in their professional abilities than men are—even when their skills are equal to or better than their male colleagues. We've all heard stories about men who have stepped up for jobs and been promoted with half the skills and experience that their women peers have. They see the promotion as an opportunity to jump forward and figure that they'll be able to handle whatever the position entails—or get the resources to do so. The head of a women's professional group spells it out this way: "Men would tend to apply for jobs if they had 30 percent of the job requirements. Women would not apply unless they had 100 percent." Men just are not as self-critical as women, who analyze and worry about whether their qualifications fit the job precisely. The study reinforces that most women are not socialized to have the "killer instinct" to take risks and compete with everything they have for top positions and the power that goes with them.

The earlier story of Jim and Donna, and their boss Roy, could have had a different ending entirely:

Timing. If Donna had stepped into the conversation earlier to express her interest in the initiative, things might have turned out differently. While she was mulling it over, she could have bought some time by saying, "That sounds like something I'd be interested in." Even when she was usurped by Jim, she still had a chance to say, "Roy, I also feel very qualified and would like to lead the project with Jim."

Positioning. If Donna had routinely let her boss know about her accomplishments, she might have been the one he thought of for the project without opening it up to the group. Remember, it's your individual responsibility to keep the boss informed about your successes on an ongoing basis.

Voice and Language. If Donna had expressed her interest in the project during the meeting, she should have been assertive and positive as she did so. Enthusiasm, too, can take you a long way—people can relate to your excitement and, even if a little boasting surfaces, it can be forgiven.

Presence. If Donna had firmly established her presence and leadership qualities with the group, Jim's play for position might have been viewed negatively by those in the meeting. In fact, they would have expected her to step up and assert her own qualifications and would have supported her, if not recommended her in the first place.

Anna, a top sales executive at a major television station, told me that she was very uncomfortable promoting herself to her boss's boss and the station manager, both men. She was careful with what she said and how she said it. She was concerned about appearing to "jump the gun" if she talked about a deal that wasn't definite. She was worried that she would be considered "too emotional" if she appeared excited about a new account. So, she kept her self-promotion on a formal level, unable to develop a comfortable style of publicizing her day-to-day successes to the executives higher up in her office. It was a totally different story with her immediate boss, a woman with whom she had a great relationship. Anna made a point of regularly stopping into her boss's office to share interim successes with new sales prospects, and when she landed a big account, she and her boss frequently shared the excitement with a hug. One of the major downsides of Anna's situation is that if her immediate boss doesn't promote her, or leaves for another job, no one else will know about her accomplishments and she will be, at least temporarily, stranded.

How good are you at promoting yourself? Take the quiz and see.

How well do you promote yourself?	*Yes*	*No*
1. Do you meet with your boss at least every six months to review accomplishments and assure alignment with his/her goals?	☐	☐
2. Do you have a list of your major accomplishments, and the skills you used to achieve them, in your desk drawer?	☐	☐
3. Have you identified the gaps in your experience and sought opportunities to gain missing skills?	☐	☐
4. Do you plan your participation in each high-level meeting you attend by analyzing issues to be discussed in advance and determining where you can add value?	☐	☐
5. Have you determined what your superiors' interests are and sent them relevant articles or e-mails periodically?	☐	☐
6. Do you copy your boss on communications to your team so that he or she will know your achievements and be able to observe your leadership style?	☐	☐
7. Do you actively try to weave your accomplishments into stories as appropriate?	☐	☐
8. Are you prepared to promote your accomplishments and take on new opportunities when they arise?	☐	☐
9. Have you established good relationships with your superiors so they feel comfortable with you and your style?	☐	☐

If you answered yes to six or more questions, you are making strides in promoting yourself. Congratulations! Fewer than six means you may not be doing enough to be a visible candidate for a promotion or career opportunity that comes up. Think about the strategies you can use to better position yourself with peers and superiors and help them feel more comfortable with you.

Sometimes, the woman you least expect to lack confidence surprises you. Nan, who is head of a sales division for a major pharmaceutical company, has a strong voice, commanding presence, and successful track record. At least, that's what people see on the outside. In a coaching session, when she started to analyze her career, it became clear that her exterior persona hid her insecurity. When she was asked to give a two-minute description of her strengths and accomplishments, she froze. She wasn't comfortable touting her experience. It became evident that self-confidence issues were the reason she was reluctant—she was uncertain about her talents and whether she deserved to be promoted. Nan, looked up to by most of her colleagues, secretly feared she would be uncovered as a fraud or inadequate if she talked in depth about her career accomplishments.

After spending time reviewing her peak accomplishments and analyzing all the skills she'd used to make them happen, she began to feel more confident about herself. She realized that she had already proven herself as competent and successful. Nan came to understand that she really *was* the person others admired, and began to turn her focus onto being an effective leader and promoting herself more broadly within the company.

Do you find that your lack of self-confidence interferes with your ability to talk up your work? Are you uncomfortable discussing your successes? Believe it or not, the more you promote yourself, the easier it gets. Self-promotion is not only an important quality for you as an individual, but it's vital in your role as the leader of a team. The more you promote yourself and your initiatives, the better it is for the individuals who work with you. They'll benefit, too, through your efforts, and become recognized in the organization as part of a winning team.

Tip: Praising Others Promotes You as Well

Promoting yourself and praising your team leads to better recognition for all. A true leader routinely assists talented people who work with her to attain bigger jobs, sometimes even surpassing her. It takes a secure and confident person to do this and is, in fact, another form of self-promotion. By broadening your sponsorship of people, you are promoting yourself as a leader to work for—to your staff, to colleagues, and to the people who are higher up in the organization.

How to Put Your Best Self Forward

You can demonstrate your expertise in an effective, subtle way—and still get the point across.

- Make a list of the *skills* you use to achieve your work successes and accomplishments. Update the list regularly to keep your skills in the forefront of your mind. Be ready to refer to them whenever the opportunity presents itself.
- Link your skills to your *experience* and the major accomplishments you have achieved in your career. Describe each accomplishment in a sen-

tence or two—even with few words, you can establish credibility with your audience.

- Demonstrate your qualities of *leadership* and don't be afraid to use the "I" word. An example is, "I led a wonderful project team. We did great work in increasing productivity." By starting out saying "I," it is immediately clear that, while you are giving your team credit, you are the leader.

- Do not brag or insert yourself inappropriately, but rather represent yourself in a positive way at opportune times. Promote yourself with finesse and subtlety and people will respect and admire you for it!

Kimberly was interviewing for a senior position in a consulting firm. Though she had similar job experience in another industry, her qualifications were not a perfect match. In spite of this, she was self-confident and comfortable with her accomplishments, convinced that she would be able to smoothly transfer her skills to the new organization. She sold herself, explaining why this was the right position for her—and when it was suggested that she start at a lower level in order to prove herself, she held firm. She repeated her qualifications, elaborating on the value she brought to the firm and why she was ready for a more senior position. She emphasized the revenues she could bring in. She held her confidence all the way through the interviewing process, and eventually was awarded the position. The lesson? Kimberly believed in herself, kept her cool, and stuck to her guns. She did an excellent job in linking her skills to the position available, and she stayed on message, even when her experience was questioned.

Know What You're Promoting

It is vital for a woman to fully understand her top interests, skills, talents, strengths, and experiences and to know how and when to use the information. Let's create some promotional stories by thinking about some of *your* accomplishments—something you have enjoyed doing, did well, and found satisfying.

Understanding My Accomplishments

Spend some time thinking about your career accomplishments, then list three of them on the next page. Don't be modest! This is not the time to be shy about what you accomplished. First, take a look at this example.

Accomplishment Example

My team and I introduced a major product that we had been testing for about six months because we felt it could boost company revenues. I obtained agreement on the strategic and tactical plan, presented it to management, and won approval for the budget necessary to launch the product.

Now you try it. Remember, this is a work accomplishment you enjoyed doing, did well, and found satisfying.

Accomplishment #1:

Accomplishment #2:

Accomplishment #3:

Ask yourself: "What did I do to make this accomplishment happen?" List the strengths it took to achieve your accomplishments. Moving back to the accomplishment example, the strengths you would list are:

1. I *planned* the approach.
2. I *communicated* with my team and management.
3. I *marketed* my idea.
4. I *created* a budget.
5. I *sold* the concept.

Other examples of strengths include: analyzed, identified, marketed, motivated, negotiated, persuaded, planned, resolved, sold, trained, communicated, and wrote.

Now, make your list based upon the three accomplishments. What have you learned about your skills and strengths? How many showed up in all three accomplishments? Use this exercise to catalogue and better understand your personal portfolio of skills and strengths and the role they played in your accomplishments. You'll find that these skills, which you used in the work you enjoyed, did well, and found satisfying, will surface again and again in most of your accomplishments.

Accomplishment #1

What did I do to make this happen?

1.

2.

3.

4.

5.

Accomplishment #2

What did I do to make this happen?

1.

2.

3.

4.

5.

Accomplishment #3

What did I do to make this happen?

1.

2.

3.

4.

5.

In addition, think about your core technical skills. These are skills you have learned on the job and do well, such as cost accounting, development, finance, mergers, public relations, sales training, and strategic planning.

My Core Technical Skills

1.

2.

3.

4.

5.

Now, using the previous exercises, create one or two sentences that you can use to promote yourself when the opportunity arises. Here's an example from a lawyer in a corporate setting: "I am head of the litigation department for my company and have negotiated hundreds of lawsuits, which saved my company millions of dollars in legal fees. I frequently represent the company by speaking at legal conferences about our experience with these issues, giving us a reputation as one of the leaders in our industry."

These two sentences demonstrate experience and skills in law, negotiations, speaking and public relations, and leadership. It is a jam-packed, powerful illustration of how to link your skills with your experiences.

Now it's your turn to create a sentence or two about yourself. Remember to note an accomplishment and link it with your skills as well as your technical knowledge.

I am...

How did you do? Having your strengths and skills catalogued in your mind and at the tip of your tongue prepares you to be ready even at the most unexpected times—and places. Dora was in the produce section of the supermarket when an important business associate appeared next to her. After exchanging greetings, he said, "How's it going at work?" She could have just said, "Fine," and left it at that, but, because her strengths and skills were clear in her mind, Dora was able to take the opportunity to talk about her role at work, telling him a little about her successes with a high-profile project she was leading. You never know when you need to be "on call."

Tip: Practice Tooting Your Horn

Use your promotional script and prepare anecdotes about your latest project or biggest deal so you can bring them up in conversation and make a powerful impression. Drop stories about your successes into the next conversation you have with your peers. This will help you develop a new mind-set and get used to impressing colleagues, your boss, and even an audience if you are making a presentation.

Develop a Comfortable Promotional Style

Women should develop their own unique brand of self-promotion—one that enhances their style. Emma, a very senior well-known leader in the health-care industry, is a popular speaker at regional and national conferences because of her authority and knowledge. In her role as a speaker, she always takes the opportunity to promote her health-care company and position as a senior executive by saying, "In my position as head of the mid-Atlantic division of my company, I find I have both the opportunity and resources to address some of the critical issues affecting our regional and national health care." When in meetings at her company, she invariably promotes her speaking accomplishments by saying something like, "While in Chicago as keynote speaker for the Universal Health Forum, we discussed the same topic that's on the table today." There is no mistaking who she is and the power she holds, but she promotes herself, and her company, in a way that is comfortable for her and appropriate to her position and the occasion. She speaks anecdotally, underscoring her skills and accomplishments, and linking them to whatever she wants to promote at the time, such as her job position or recognition as a speaker. This technique of self-promotion works well for many women.

Ideally, discussing one's skills and experience should come comfortably and naturally. So, try to develop a style that is comfortable for you. Imagine you're at a fund-raising event for community youth programs and are in a conversation with a couple of people who are talking about the organization.

The first thing to do is get into the conversation by saying: "Yes, I've heard about the work you're doing in this organization and think it's great. Can you tell me more about it?"

You have related to those around you, who go on talking about some specific points, after which you can say: "That's an interesting point. When I sat on a committee of the board for Another Worthwhile Youth organization, I noticed that . . ."

You've made the point that you are knowledgeable and are on a board committee of another important organization. The conversation about youth programs proceeds and you say: "I remember exactly when I got interested in this. As head of human resources for ABC Company, I am responsible for hiring the summer interns . . . "

Now, you've shown that you are an executive of a well-known company. You continue talking with your group, and perhaps end by saying: "I'd love to talk with you further about this sometime."

Think of the conversation as providing a number of openings to connect with others, establish your credibility, and offer value. This technique allows you to use various opportunities to "layer in" more information in an appropriate and comfortable way. Try it at your next networking event and adapt it to your individual circumstances. If you don't have board experience, for example, you might mention that you've read up on the organization.

Tip: Focus on the One You're With

Have you ever been in a conversation at an event with someone who appears to be distracted, and continuously scans the room as if they're looking to find someone more important to talk to? It's terribly insulting, and a definite no-no. Always focus on the people you're with until you leave the conversation by making a tactful exit. For example, you can say, "Please excuse me. A client of mine just came in" or "I'll see you a little later—I'm going to get something to eat." Always make the person you're with feel that you consider them important—and then go on to circulate with others.

Since most women have not been trained to "toot their own horn," promoting yourself may feel like boasting or bragging. There are, however, real differences between bragging and bringing up your skills in conversation. Most of the time, when you perceive someone is "bragging," it is because whatever they're saying seems like it's out of context. They've brought it up for the sole purpose of making themselves seem important, smart, wealthy, or powerful. They often talk loudly, looking around for a reaction from others, and there is usually an air of self-absorption and presumption in what they are conveying.

This is not an effective way of demonstrating your expertise. Here are some phrases that, though they say virtually the same thing, come across to the listener very differently.

The Language of Self-Promoting versus Bragging

Bragging...	*Self-promoting...*
I made this deal happen . . .	While leading the team, I was able to bring this deal together . . .
I've got the best way to . . .	One way that's worked for me . . .
You must try this . . .	I was so happy with the results, you should give it a try . . .
I'm a shoo-in for this promotion . . .	I believe I have all the skills for this new position . . .
They couldn't have done it without me . . .	I enjoyed having a pivotal role on that . . .

See—you *can* promote yourself without bragging!

It's important to know, and be conscious of, how the decision makers in your company view self-promotion. Be sure your conduct is in sync with their unstated rules. Lilly, vice president of a local marketing company, should have understood the unwritten corporate message: only the CEO of her firm was to be in the spotlight. She got into trouble when she got a call from a reporter who was doing a story about a high-profile project she was involved in. She talked with him, thinking it was good promotion for the company and for herself. But, she neglected to mention it to the CEO and when the article ran in a widely distributed newsletter along with her photo, he was steaming. Even though it was not something Lilly initiated or planned, guess who didn't speak to her for the next three months? It made for an uncomfortable situation with her boss, to say the least. If she'd truly been in tune with her CEO (and his ego), she could have handled it differently. She would have put the reporter in touch with the CEO after she filled in the background and details, so they both would get the publicity. That way, she would have promoted herself and earned some credits with the boss.

Take Every Opportunity

At a recent professional meeting, the members decided that each would take ten minutes to update everyone on their progress, goals, and business. They started at one point in the room and went person by person to get updates from everyone. They hadn't gotten around to Nancy, who was at the far end of the room and had to leave early for another meeting. Nancy gathered her papers together and, just before another person's report was about to start, she spoke up and said, "Unfortunately I have another commitment and will have to leave shortly. Would it be okay for me to give my update now?" Everyone agreed, and Nancy stood, knowing that after her report she would exit the room. It was a perfect opportunity for her to speak with a commanding presence because she was on her feet. As she was finishing, another member added some positive comments about a project Nancy had done that she had heard good things about, and Nancy thanked her for the support. Nancy made the most of the meeting. By asking to speak to the group before she left, she got the benefit of their attention to her report, as well as "endorsement" from another member.

It is especially important and necessary for women to support and promote other women in their efforts to succeed. The prominent editor of a women's magazine, who was the speaker at a meeting of four hundred senior businesswomen, stated firmly, "If you are sitting alone at the top of your organization with no other woman at your level or right behind you, nipping at your heels to get ahead—make no mistake, you're a token." At that time, most of the women in the room were alone at their senior levels and had few women directly below them. In their race to climb the ladder in their companies, many of them had eliminated other women as competitors. This has to change. In order for the cultures of our companies to change, women have to help other women so the numbers change at the top. By supporting fellow women, you can affect progress for all of us. One way to do this within your organization is to get a group of women together and have them join forces to help each other advance instead of being in competition with one another. They can advise each other, promote agendas, even protest injustices together—and everyone benefits.

Another way to have others promote you is to enlist the support of a boss or mentor with whom you have a good relationship. Be confident enough to tell him or her what you're looking for in your next career step and ask for help and advice. In the best case scenario, they will become invested in your success and be on the lookout for opportunities for you. Imagine meetings where you are not present. If your boss or mentor is aware of what you've done and what you want, he or she can speak up on your behalf. If he or she doesn't know your ambitions, you've lost out.

There are a number of ways to be promoted by others. Remember, though, you need to be sure that the people who are promoting and supporting you know enough about your skills and accomplishments. If they are familiar with these, there are many different occasions when they can jump in and be your supporter.

Five Ways to Have Others Promote You

1. *When you're in the room*: If you have good, strong relationships with colleagues, they are more likely to show support for you in a meeting. When a discussion arises on who should lead a project or who has expertise in a specific area, colleagues who know your skills and respect your work can promote you by saying, "You have a lot of experience in this area too, don't you? You worked on the XYZ project." At which point, you can jump in the conversation and promote yourself.
2. *When you're not present*: Let's return to the same situation as above, except this time you're not at the meeting, you're on vacation. Assuming the others in the meeting are familiar with your background, skills, accomplishments, and goals—and feel loyal to you for past support—your associates can talk about how your experience and skills fit into the new project. The boss just might hold off on making any decision about the person to head the project until she or he has spoken to you.
3. *From inside your company to the outside business community*: If the key people within your company know your work and you've told them of your interests, they are more likely to think of you. For example, if you've told your boss about your interest in getting involved in outside professional activities to expand your experience, he or she is more likely to think of you for a committee of a professional association when an opening comes up.
4. *From the outside business community to your company*: The reverse of the previous example is a situation in which you're active and involved outside of your company and meet people who know your boss or colleagues. As you become known to them, they are likely to tell your boss or colleague that they know you through a civic group and that you're doing a great job.
5. *By setting up your own networking group*: You can gather your own contacts and friends and form a group for the sole purpose of helping each other in the business community. Each person will need to be supportive of the others and agreeable to the "rules" of the group so there are no competitive conflicts.

Think about those around you who can help support and promote you. You'll find that developing a strategy around these key individuals will keep you focused. The worksheet below is for just that purpose. Keep in mind that opportunities often come forth when you're not around.

My Personal Marketing Strategy for Key Supporters (example)

Name of Key Supporter: My boss, Jim
Title: Vice President

1. **How I'd like our relationship to be**: To know each other better on a more casual level. For him to feel comfortable enough with me to ask my advice and opinion.
2. **Assessment of how it is now**:

   Strengths: He seems to appreciate my work.
   Weaknesses: He never drops in my office or asks me to join him for lunch.
   What I have working for me: In-depth knowledge of my work and our department through prior experience with a competitor.

Description of my goals:

   Long-range: To be on his executive team and a key member of the group.
   Short-range: To demonstrate my knowledge through my work and participation in an upcoming project.

Description of my strategy:

- To arrange a meeting to discuss my current work (and prior experience!)
- To drop in more frequently and update him
- To volunteer on specific projects he's involved with

What do I need?

- More time with him to develop the relationship
- Knowledge of his interests
- Access to him (crossing paths)

Description of possible roadblocks:
He seems a little uncomfortable with women and I rarely see him with women colleagues. All of his other direct reports are men he goes to lunch with. I intend to make him feel at ease with me.

My first step:
Set up a meeting to review my progress.

1. Now, select a couple of people you would like to get to know better who can help you in your self-promotion strategy and complete your worksheet for each!

My Personal Marketing Strategy for Key Supporters

Name of Key Supporter:
Title:

1. **How I'd like our relationship to be:**

   Assessment of how it is now:

   Strengths:
   Weaknesses:
   What I have working for me:

2. **Description of my goals:**

   Long-range:
   Short-range:

3. **Description of my strategy:**

4. **What do I need?**

5. **Description of possible roadblocks:**

6. **My first step:**

You're ready now to follow through on the plan above.

Tip: **Make an Impression**

Take the initiative to ask for a performance review. Although your stated meeting purpose is to be sure your work is on point, you can also use the meeting to communicate your strengths and accomplishments. Be ready and able to talk about your projects and achievements and ask how things are going from your manager's point of view. The result? You'll get good feedback and suggestions, and make a memorable impression.

Spread the Word

In order to get others to help you promote yourself, it's important to get the word out on anything significant that's happened to you—achievements, awards, and accomplishments. So, if something good happens, don't be shy, tell people. Especially people you consider well-placed and who would be interested. Why? They'll pass it along to others and soon you'll be receiving calls about your achievement instead of initiating them.

Let's say you receive a promotion at work. After you call your significant other, parents, and best friend, think about key people in your network to whom this would be interesting, pertinent information. Then call to tell them. Perhaps they've given you advice in the past, or been supportive of your career. You could say, "I wanted to tell you about this because you've been so helpful to me."

Now, they feel a part of your success and are even more apt to pass on the story. An additional benefit of telling key players is that you are able to give the true story so the information "on the street" will be accurate. In essence, you're being your own public relations person.

Your ability to get noticed and get ahead by selling your strengths rests in large part on understanding your own strengths and telling your story. As you go about "marketing" yourself, think about what you want others to know about you. What do you want them to think of when your name comes up? What personal and professional attributes do you want them to associate you with? What should they be updated about?

Keep your message fresh and current as you:

- Remind people of what your goals are.
- Ask to be involved in high-visibility projects.

- Get assignments done well and on time.
- Be available when people need you.
- Stay in front of people.
- Develop your own style of self-promotion.
- Tell others what you're working on.

When you begin to think of self-promotion as a positive force, and develop a style that is comfortable for you, it will make a big difference in your career. As you and your accomplishments are known by more influential people, you will gain a stronger foothold in your organization, become better known in your community, and the door will open to many more career possibilities.

Learn the Rules, Play the Game
Navigate the Politics of
Your Corporate Culture

O MANY WOMEN, "political" sounds like the dark side of the corporate world, and they think that to be good at corporate politicking means using others and abusing power. It represents the ultimate in putting one's own interests first at the expense of others and breaches, for many women, a basic code of conduct. Senior women in a recent research study talked positively about "collaboration" and "sharing of information" and observed that women are more "depoliticized, not much into game playing" and that they "don't see or use issues as turf battles." The truth is, when executed correctly, political savvy is not about backstabbing and lying but, in fact, relies on being collaborative, sharing information, and doing what's right for the organization.

Marion, one of the most visible business leaders and activists in her community, is a model of political savvy at its best. She's on a number of boards and heads a large civic organization. When a controversial issue arises, she is careful not to polarize groups that have differing agendas. She looks at what is needed and what will work, and remains flexible, trying to find positives on each side of an issue without strongly aligning herself with one side or another. In this way, she is able to neutralize the negative and move her agenda forward. She is highly thought of in the community, is called upon to solve some of its thorniest issues, and has an uncanny ability to get things accomplished with most people thinking she's "on their side," regardless of their agendas or political leanings. In order to get your good ideas adopted, affect organizational change, become recognized, and be promoted, you'll need to understand how to navigate your organization and become politically astute. Otherwise, you will find your great ideas going nowhere.

Being politically savvy is really about building alliances in order to get things done. If you decide, for example, you want to effect a change in your company or drive an initiative, or maybe you just thought of "the next big idea," what do you do? If your answer is, "Run into my boss's office and tell him my big idea," you are *not* being politically savvy!

Susan did it the right way. She is a vice president in the financial services industry and, as an avid reader of trade publications and magazines, she took notice of research in *American Demographics* magazine showing that women control more than 60 percent of the wealth in the country and that, in twenty-five years, 95 percent of women will manage their own finances. It struck her that it might make sense for her bank to focus on marketing financial services to women. By doing so, she reasoned, they would appeal to this large market in a unique way and could distinguish themselves from their competitors. She started building corroborating evidence by pulling together some facts and figures starting with the research statistics and adding her own observations and experience. She then planned to see what others in her organization said, build a base of support for the idea, and begin to determine its potential impact to the bank's bottom line.

After doing her research, Susan met with each of her colleagues to run the idea by them and get their input and support. She then set up an appointment with her boss, picking a time when he appeared to be in a good mood and things were going well, to present her idea. She had carefully prepared the research to build her case, done the competitive analysis, listed the pros and cons, and calculated the costs and projected financial return of developing a women's initiative. Her boss was impressed with her thoroughness, and decided to take the idea to the next level, where he encountered support from people who had heard about the idea.

It would have been naïve of Susan to think that sharing an idea, no matter how good, without context or support and with only one individual, even her boss, would lead to success. Susan took the time to think strategically about her idea, and do her homework—and it paid off.

Tip: **Time It Right**

When you are enthusiastic about an idea, your tendency is to want to share it immediately. Resist the urge! Instead of blurting out your idea, stop and decide whether the timing is right to present your grand plan to your boss. Is he or she distracted with another, more urgent situation? Is he preoccupied with problems at home? Did she just receive bad news? Before you let your excitement dictate your timing, use your intuitive powers and make sure conditions are as favorable as possible for presenting your idea.

Take this quiz to see how your political savvy stacks up:

Are you politically savvy?	Yes	No
1. Do you think strategically about how to move forward with an idea or initiative?	☐	☐
2. Do you informally research an idea to get relevant background information?	☐	☐
3. Do you take time to talk with colleagues about ideas and initiatives to get buy-in and support for your ideas?	☐	☐
4. Do you analyze who the organizational and project decision makers are and where they stand on an issue?	☐	☐
5. Have you thought about what they may gain, personally and professionally, from the success of your initiative?	☐	☐
6. Do you have a good understanding of the people in your organization who influence the decision makers?	☐	☐
7. Do you know how the influencers feel about ideas you want to present, and why they hold that opinion?	☐	☐
8. Do you do your homework before you present an idea?	☐	☐

If you answered yes to five or more of these questions, you are politically astute about pushing forward your agenda! If not, you have some work to do in order to become more effective in your organization.

Collaboration Is Key

Collaboration with others, often a strong suit for women, is vital to getting your ideas moved ahead. If you think about it, you'll realize how often you need not only support from others in your organization to make things happen, but also their technical knowledge, expertise, and perspective. For example, Laura is a marketing director in a large manufacturing company, and part of her job entails spending time on the road with Sam, the sales director. Traditionally the marketing and sales divisions have had preconceived—and often negative—ideas about the other. Clearly, Laura and Sam were competitors, not buddies, and often seemed to come to issues from different directions. During one of their road trips, they saw a piece of machinery that struck both of them as a great possibility in opening up a new market for their company. Laura and Sam realized that the idea had enormous potential—and that putting their differences aside and joining forces gave them a better chance of success and the recognition that would come with it.

So, they laid the groundwork for their idea by doing preliminary research and profit projections, and they scheduled a meeting with their bosses to get their thoughts and ideas. Both men liked the idea and Laura and Sam got a green light to continue, as well as some valuable advice on how to proceed. With the backing of their superiors, they received additional resources to put together a comprehensive development plan to be presented to the executive committee. The plan, which included the endorsement of the sales and marketing divisions, was accepted and resulted in a highly successful new product line that doubled its volume in the first year. Laura and Sam were politically smart and reaped the rewards of their collaborative effort. They saw the bigger picture—and instead of sniping at each other, built an alliance that produced a positive result for them and the company.

Tip: Keep Your Enemies Close

Join forces with your archenemy—the person who beat you out for that project you wanted so badly. Though you've not seen eye to eye and, in fact, you don't like her much, when you have a common interest, it's wise to enlist her support. If you have a goal you both would like to see accomplished, put the past aside and approach her with your plan. It will work to the benefit of both of you. Remember, though, she's not your friend, just a convenient political ally, so keep your guard up. There's an old saying to remember: "Having a relationship with an alligator is fine, as long as his (or her) mouth stays closed."

The Road Map to Move Your Project Forward

Let's say you want to introduce an organizational change to produce better results or drive an initiative that could save your company millions. Though you may have great ideas, you need the help of others. The first thing to do is develop a strategy for getting your project or idea accomplished by analyzing who the ultimate decision maker is, where he or she stands on the issue, and who are the people who influence him or her. In other words, you need to *understand the big picture of all the people who need to support your idea, and create a plan of attack.*

Here's an example of how to work through the political issues on a project. Let's say Kim has an idea for the company and she's done her homework on the pros and cons, history, competition, and market landscape. Now, she wants to move the idea forward with the key players.

Kim's Project Planner

> **Idea**: My idea is a new accounting procedure to keep track of individual company subsidiary expenses.
> **Important Background Information**: Has never been done by the organization. Subsidiary numbers are now combined and rolled up into one number.
> **Final Decision Maker**: Corporate Chief Financial Officer
> **Decision Maker's Possible Gain**: Would help him run his area more effectively. By identifying individual subsidiary numbers, he could target specific companies and reduce expenses.
> **Key Influencers**: The VP of Finance who reports to the CFO is a big influencer and has the CFO's attention and respect. So is the CEO, who is the CFO's boss. It is likely the CFO will run a final decision by the CEO before deciding. Two of my peers are good friends of the VP of Finance.
> **Winners/Losers**: Corporate headquarters executives would be winners because they could track costs of each of the subsidiary companies. Some of the presidents of subsidiaries would be happy to track their costs more precisely, but others would feel threatened because their numbers would be revealed and open to scrutiny.

Analysis

Kim has identified the people who would have major influence over the decisions necessary to implement her idea. When you have a number of people influencing the decision, it's sometimes helpful to chart them to determine where they fall:

- Are they positive, negative, or neutral?
- Who outranks whom?
- Who do you know well?
- If you don't know the key influencer, who do you know who knows the key influencer?

Below is an example of how to plot the individuals influencing the decision. The left side shows the people who have a negative opinion, the right side shows supporters, with the middle as neutral. The people with the highest level positions are toward the top.

Where Do the Influencers Stand?

CEO

Subsidiary Presidents 1 & 2   CFO   Subsidiary Presidents 3 & 4

Peer 1   VP Finance   Peer 2

(-)   △   (+)

- The CEO is the highest ranking decision maker, so he tops the chart. Because he doesn't yet know about the idea, we start by categorizing his stance as neutral. Kim will need to move him to the positive for the idea to succeed.
- The CFO is one step below in rank, although we consider him the "final decision maker" for the idea. Again, we've categorized him as neutral, but Kim must move him to a very positive position in order to push the idea through with the subsidiary presidents.
- Next in rank are the subsidiary presidents and, at the outset, Kim has ranked two (numbers 1 and 2) as negative and two (numbers 3 and 4) as positive, based on her knowledge of their working styles and preferences. Through discussion with each of them, she hopes to move the negatives to either neutral or positive, and to retain the positives.

- The VP of Finance is close in ranking to the subsidiary presidents and, as far as Kim knows, is also neutral. Since Kim hopes that he will serve as an advocate for her idea, she must move him to the positive side.
- Kim's peers, whom she has supported in the past, will be asked to be advocates. After a brief discussion, she ranks one more positive than the other. The objective is for both of them to be very positive after discussing the idea with Kim.

After plotting the key players, Kim starts to implement her plan to advocate for her idea so that she can move as many decision makers as possible to the positive side of her chart.

- First, Kim met with her two peers, who are also good friends, and filled them in on her idea and its benefits, where she thought everyone stood, and, most important, how they could return a favor by talking with the VP of Finance. They generally liked the idea she presented, offered a couple of suggestions, and told her they would each mention it favorably to the VP of Finance and report back to her.
- Kim arranged a lunch to broach the idea directly with the VP of Finance. She outlined the proposed system and its benefits to both corporate headquarters and the subsidiaries. She also wove into the discussion the ways in which the system would increase his ability to provide valuable information to the CFO and CEO. The VP asked a number of questions, made some valuable suggestions about how to approach the subsidiary presidents, and said he would run the idea by his boss, the CFO. Kim set up meetings with the subsidiary presidents to get their input. She then let her peers know that she would appreciate their support.
- She then set up appointments with each of the subsidiary presidents and presented her idea, asking them for their thoughts and advice. She received a cool reception from number 1, a neutral acceptance from number 2, and highly positive reactions from numbers 3 and 4.
- She reported back to the VP of Finance, who said his trial balloon with the CFO had been a success—the CFO was interested enough to set up a time for himself, the CEO, the VP of Finance, and Kim to more formally discuss the idea and how best to implement it.

So far, so good! Kim and her idea are on their way. Her chart has changed to reflect the outcomes of these meetings and now looks like this:

Where Do the Influencers Stand? (Updated)

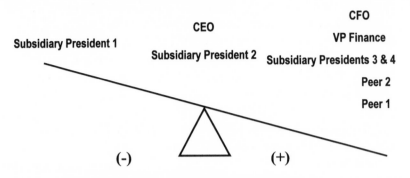

You can now clearly see what Kim was able to do:

- She moved the peer who was on the negative side to the positive.
- Both peers advocated with the VP of Finance, who eventually moved into positive territory too.
- Though Subsidiary President 1 remained unmoved, number 2 was neutralized.
- Finally, and most important, all of this groundwork resulted in moving the CFO into a positive stance resulting in his willingness to take the idea to the CEO. Ultimately, the CEO was impressed with Kim's idea and the project got off the ground.

Now think of an idea or initiative you would like to take on in your company. Draw your own chart for your idea. You'll probably end up with a lot of arrows as you move people from one side to the other. You'll need to add people who influence the decision makers or who influence the influencers.

First, let's review the steps you can take to put your plan in motion:

10 Steps to a Successful Initiative

Step 1:   Uncover background information and history that may impact your project.

Step 2:   Analyze who stands to gain—and lose.

Step 3:   Float the idea by key players to gauge reaction, get input, and gain support.

Step 4:   Determine who the real decision maker is.

Step 5:   Find out what he or she will personally and professionally gain from success.

Step 6:   Establish who influences the decision maker.

Step 7:   Find out what the influencers' individual positions are and who knows them.

Step 8:   Develop a plan for addressing the decision maker and each key influencer.

Step 9:   Listen to others' thoughts and ideas and make appropriate adjustments to the concept.

Step 10:   Thank each individual for his or her input, and circle back to update them on the status of your initiative.

Now, try it for your own initiative after you complete the *project planner* outline.

My Project Planner

Idea:

Important Background Information:

Final Decision Maker:

Decision Maker's Possible Gain:

Key Influencers:

Winners/Losers:

Analysis:

Now take a moment to plot where you think your key influencers stand on the above idea.

Where Do *Your* Key Influencers Stand?

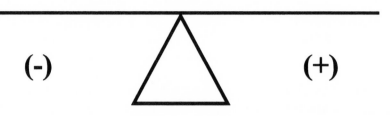

$$(-) \qquad\qquad (+)$$

Once you've thought about all the players who will have an impact on the success of your idea—and their agendas—you will be able to take steps to move forward on your initiative.

When considering the players, one person whose agenda you'll want to take into account is the lone senior woman who regards herself as the "trailblazer." Many companies have one—you may have encountered her. She's been at the company for years and has advanced into the executive ranks even though she doesn't represent the ideal leadership model. When another woman is hired or promoted to the senior ranks, the trailblazer can become anxious and insecure about her role. Be careful to neutralize any negative feelings by paying special attention to her and considering her viewpoint. She's got a history with people and you want her to feel comfortable with you.

Tip: Find Out Who Can Make or Break You

*Be clever in determining who **really** impacts on your success. Use your powers of observation to map out who plays golf or goes to lunch with whom, which employees an executive has brought on board from a former company, and, the ultimate bond, who went to school together. Then develop your strategy for seeking out the key players and building relationships with them. Your future depends on it!*

Sometimes your plans for a relationship don't quite pan out. When that occurs, it's time to back off. Robin, a marketing executive in a large consumer goods company, saw that a peer on whom she depended for her own success was doing some things that had really angered some important people. The peer managed the research division of the company, which provided the data for marketing. He had, for some unknown reason, started bad-mouthing a couple of important people and selectively withholding information from them and the people who reported to them—including Robin. She could see that he was shooting himself in the foot politically and that the situation was creating problems for her. She was doubly annoyed because they had worked as allies in the past.

She had a few choices: she could join his group of company critics, try to ignore the situation, or instead, try to help him. After considering the possibilities, she decided to try to work with him, thinking that if she could improve the communication between them, she could turn the situation around. Robin reasoned that because they had worked successfully on projects in the past, if he could get beyond his current problems, they could work together successfully in the future.

So, Robin shared some feedback and information with him and made a few suggestions. Instead of listening, however, he chose to ignore her advice. She began to realize she was fighting a losing battle—he didn't want help and it was time for her to step back. Robin's fear was that his demise could impact her in a negative way, but unfortunately, she could only watch as he lost ground in the organization. Luckily for her, he left soon thereafter on his own and she was not negatively affected. When his replacement was hired, Robin began alliance building with her.

How to Play and Be Respected

You don't have to stoop to ugly tactics to be a part of the political game. You can be respected—and respectful—and still be a politically astute player in your organization and your community. In fact, these traits are likely to get you included and involved, and will help keep you in the information loop. People will want to come to you for advice and support on their projects, and you will be able to turn to them as needed. This is the ultimate in being politically savvy.

Take a look at the traits listed on the next page—are you astute, a troublemaker, or not a player at all? Check the ones that match you.

Consistency Wins

Marla's brand of political savvy was not immediately apparent to most people. As head of a department in an insurance company, she was the person everyone sought for guidance and advice. Her style was to be helpful to everyone—but she was much more than just "nice." She was extremely astute

An Astute Player

- ☐ Communicates tactfully
- ☐ Listens to others
- ☐ Works on relationships
- ☐ Has a great sense of key players
- ☐ Knows when to step back
- ☐ Understands the culture
- ☐ Picks his/her battles
- ☐ Builds alliances
- ☐ Is flexible
- ☐ Has interests of the company in mind

If you've checked off six or more, you are politically astute. If you've checked fewer than six, you have more work to do.

A Manipulative Troublemaker

- ☐ Talks at people
- ☐ Abuses power
- ☐ Uses people
- ☐ Plays up to superiors
- ☐ Has a do-or-die attitude
- ☐ Backstabs, ignores, and goes around coworkers
- ☐ Takes advantage at others' expense
- ☐ Undercuts others
- ☐ Is rigid
- ☐ Puts his/her own agenda first

You didn't *really* check off more than two, did you? If you did, you need to think about your tactics—it sounds like you've got some bad habits.

Not a Player at All

☐ Keeps to himself/herself

☐ Doesn't care about power

☐ Has few relationships

☐ Doesn't know key players

☐ Never thinks about alliances

☐ Ignores the culture

☐ Says whatever comes to mind

☐ Has no plan

☐ Is oblivious to others

☐ Doesn't go out of his/her way

If you've checked off more than three, it sounds like you're not in the game. You need to think about the big picture and what you need to do to become a player.

---

and knew that the more she helped others, the more they would be willing to help her in return. One of the other department heads who was very knowledgeable was not well-liked because he was introverted, unkempt, and difficult to deal with. Marla, however, went out of her way to befriend him, knowing that his expertise was invaluable. They developed an amicable relationship that was built on mutual respect, and they helped each other out whenever possible. You would have to say that Marla was a political person, but the people she knew never felt used or manipulated because they were treated with respect. Marla wasn't a phony—she was politically smart and, ultimately, everyone benefited.

To be politically astute, it is important to establish a consistent style of behavior, like Marla did. If you are known as a person who is consistently collaborative and respectful of others, when you need to enlist them for a political reason, you will not be seen as Machiavellian. In the example above, Marla's style was to help others and, when she asked for their help, they were happy to comply. You'll want to assess your own style and behavior as you hone your political skills.

Do a Culture Check

Each organization has its own personality and reputation, which usually starts at the top and permeates down and heavily influences how individuals view others and behave toward their coworkers. For example, some companies are more political than others, and even departments or divisions within a company can sometimes be identified as having a more "game-playing" reputation. Each organization has an unstated protocol on how decisions are made, and has its own rules on things like who mingles with whom, how high a profile to maintain, and how meetings are run. Do you know the culture of *your* company?

What Is *Your* Company's Cultural Profile?

Rate your company on a scale of 1 to 5 on each of the following factors to understand its cultural profile. For example, is your company's culture based on Teamwork, a 5 or 4, or on Internal Competitions, a 2 or 1—or is it neutral, a 3? Circle the ones that match your company. Once you know your culture, you can choose to play within its rules—or, try to effect change within it.

You should now have a pretty good idea of your culture. If you find your philosophy is at odds with that of the organization, you may need to make some decisions. Have you worked hard on project teams only to be frustrated when all the recommendations are nixed at the top? Have you found that coworkers who consistently blame others—you included—have gotten praise and promotions, while you have not? Are you frequently confused by conflicting signals about what the priorities are and what is valued? If you determine your style is not appreciated, you have some choices. You can:

- Stick with your own approach, hoping the organization changes or those around you develop an appreciation of your style; or
- Seek a new opportunity with an organization that more closely matches your style.

Be realistic. Culture is very ingrained—and you will most likely not be the hero who effects a drastic transformation. Unless you are at the very top of the organization with a legion of loyal supporters, you will probably *not* be able to effect a massive change in the company culture or values. If you and the culture are at odds, it may be time to admit it's a bad fit and move on.

Now that you better understand your company's culture and its key players, ask yourself: With whom am I perceived as having close ties? Is that

My Company's Culture Has . . .

Internal Competitions			Teamwork/Mutual Support	
1	2	3	4	5

If your company is highly competitive, your tactics may need to be more aggressive.

Top-Down Mandates			Open Communication	
1	2	3	4	5

If mandates come directly from the top, you will need to focus your efforts on the CEO, or his or her close allies, to move an idea forward.

Lack of Alignment at Top		Alignment of Goals/Vision from Top		
1	2	3	4	5

If there is a lack of vision from the top, set an example in your group showing why collaboration is effective by creating a highly focused, fully aligned team.

Collaboration Not a Priority			Collaboration as a Focus	
1	2	3	4	5

If collaboration is not currently an organizational priority, you can still work collaboratively in meetings you attend and demonstrate its effectiveness through your own personal actions.

Finds Excuses for Failure			Accountability for Results	
1	2	3	4	5

If people around you are looking to place blame, be aware of it and make sure you don't fall into that trap yourself.

person on the "right" team within the organization? How can I build additional astute alliances?

Pay Attention to Change

It is vital to keep your ear to the ground to learn what changes are occurring within the organization's political landscape. There are times when it makes sense to look at your alliances and consider broadening them to include a wider scope of colleagues. This way, you gain by having a more varied range of possible allies and information pipelines within the organization.

Ellen had a close relationship with her boss, who was director of the consulting division of their large accounting firm and had recently promoted her to partner. She rarely took the opportunity to spend time with the managing partner of the firm, to whom her boss reported. Therefore, he hardly knew her, heard about her only through her boss, and closely connected the two. When the managing partner started to explore the possibilities of a merger, this should have been a red light for Ellen, because the firms he was talking to were larger than theirs, which meant there wouldn't be two directors of consulting and the larger player was likely to keep the position. It would have been wise of Ellen to start initiating direct contact with the managing partner and other key players immediately upon hearing of the possible merger in order to stay in the loop. She could have built important alliances and shown others that she was a talented individual worth keeping. She didn't, and when her firm was acquired, Ellen was so connected to her boss that when the decision was made for him to leave, it was practically assumed that she wouldn't want to stay and work for the new director of consulting. Ellen lost her job. She had taken the ride up the corporate elevator with her boss, but didn't get off in time.

Tip: Don't Hitch Your Wagon to One Star

It's highly unflattering to be viewed as someone's "sidekick"—and can be fatal to your career. Instead of putting yourself in this vulnerable position, make sure you have at least three strong allies in different areas of the company. Creating a broader base of alliances is a smart way to look out for yourself.

Having your boss as an ally is—more often than not—an important and necessary element to being politically savvy. Sandy was intuitive enough to sense a situation with her boss that needed some attention, and smart enough to correct it. She worked in the publicity department of a major real estate firm for several years, but her boss, with whom she had a great relationship, had been promoted several months ago and someone had been brought in from the outside to replace her, putting a layer between Sandy and her mentor. Sandy had always received excellent performance reviews, but wasn't certain about the chemistry with her new boss. While she and the new boss seemed to get along on the surface, she sensed an undercurrent of resentment from him and couldn't figure out why. After all, she was working on the projects she had always been involved in, and knew that her boss's boss was complimentary of her work. After thinking about it, she realized that her new boss might be threatened by her relationship with her previous boss, and that it would be politically astute to develop an individual relationship with the new boss, based on *his* interests and priorities.

She asked for a meeting to discuss his vision of the department and her role. Her goal was to find out more about him and what his priorities were, so she could channel her energy in the right direction. Once she realized what was important to him, she developed a positive relationship that included informal chats and occasional lunches. She continued the relationship with her boss's boss, but was careful to balance that with her present boss's need to establish himself as head of the department. She was able to successfully maintain alliances with both individuals, and when her previous boss eventually left the company, she and her new boss both moved up in the organization.

Six Tips for Playing Smart

Corporate politics is one of the areas that has proven most difficult for women in business. Even if you think, deep down, that it's distasteful and even somewhat crass, building alliances is a practical necessity. Here are some final tips that might help:

1. **See shades of gray.** In the "game" of politics, it is easy to see things as black or white, right or wrong. Instead, look for opportunities to compromise and reach a solution.
2. **Choose your battles.** If major players are starting to line up on the negative side of a project you're promoting, don't be afraid to call it quits and use your chits another day.
3. **Broaden your base of allies.** If your alliances cut across the organization, you'll have more resources to tap into, making it easier to get your ideas adopted.
4. **Keep taking the temperature of the organization.** Look for, and be ready to respond to, trends that affect the direction of your organization and may change its views—especially on any project that is your responsibility.
5. **Make sure your idea is worth pursuing.** Be sure to gauge and document the value of an idea you're promoting before you get too invested in it.

6. **Ask how you can be of help**. If you ask to be involved in projects, you will gain new information and become better known in your organization.

Being politically savvy requires balancing the needs of your organization with your own career aspirations and the goodwill of your colleagues. The fact is, if you want to be in the game, you have to understand the rules and play.

CHAPTER 5

Make the Most of a Mentor
Maximize Your Mentoring Relationships

WHEN JENNA accepted a new position as director of operations at a leading insurance company, she knew she would be the highest level woman in the office. She was well-qualified for her position and confident about her ability to shine in her new job.

Since she was new to the company and there were no women peers, however, she was somewhat apprehensive about how to break into the male-dominated bureaucracy. As Jenna began to meet with the key players in her organization, she started to get a sense of the culture and the people. But, to access the informal information channels and gain insight into the dynamics of the organization, she decided that her best course of action was to look for a mentor to help her.

Since it was vital to choose the right person, she took enough time to observe the relationships of the various players as well as their interplay in meetings. She thought about what she was looking for in a mentor and narrowed it down to someone who could provide corporate insights and information as well as strategic advice. Jenna had a couple of people in mind, both of whom she respected and felt comfortable with. One was the vice president of sales and marketing, who had been with the company for more than ten years and seemed to know everyone and everything. The second possibility was a vice president in the research area. He'd been with the company since he left graduate school, and knew a lot of early history and background information on the company.

Jenna eventually reasoned that the vice president of research was her best choice, since their chemistry was good and he seemed to be more accessible. When the timing was right, she asked him to lunch to broach the subject formally. She explained that she valued his advice and insights, especially since she was new to the company, and that she'd like him be her mentor. He was genuinely flattered and happy to help her. As Jenna moved forward at the company, the relationship worked well and made her transition easier. Later, when Jenna decided she needed help with style and communication issues, she found a senior woman in another part of her organization to be an additional mentor.

Jenna's decision to find mentors when she needed them was smart. Having the perspective of someone who is seasoned in the corporate culture and will give honest feedback is invaluable—especially when you're new to a job or company.

Everyone needs mentors to help them grow and excel—even after they reach upper management. Yet, research at The Leader's Edge has indicated mentors often serve men better than women because women regard their mentors as protective and supportive allies, while men use mentors more actively to gain visibility, promotions, and choice assignments. We, as women, need to rethink our "passive" use of mentoring relationships and how we can derive more value from mentors in terms of our career advancement.

Finding a Mentor Who's Right for You

In order to maximize a mentor relationship, you first need to think about the areas in which a mentor can be most helpful to you. Each person's situation is unique and we all have different priorities and needs.

- Do you want help in getting ahead?
- Do you stumble over the same business issues and need advice?
- Are you uncertain about your ability to read and deal with people?
- Are you having difficulty juggling your work and family?
- Do you need advice on how to enhance your skills?
- Are you interested in joining an outside board?
- Do you need exposure to another area of business?
- Do you want to emulate a mentor's style?
- Do you need someone to help you navigate the politics?

All of these issues can be addressed in a mentoring relationship and you may find that different stages of your career will bring different mentoring needs.

Mentoring at Different Career Stages

While there are core functions a mentor should provide at all organizational levels, the emphasis will probably be different as you move upward on the corporate ladder. Generally speaking, the attributes and experience you may need from a mentor at each stage of your career are:

Early Career Mentoring

What do you need from a mentor? Exposure to key players in the organization, advice on your business strategy, functional skills required for the future, and feedback on your personal style and communication.

What to look for in a mentor: A senior person in the organization with successful job/career experience, excellent leadership skills, and an effective communication style. He or she should be accessible and known for supporting younger professionals in the company.

Manager-Level Mentoring

What do you need from a mentor? Opportunities for growth and exposure through projects, initiatives, or consideration for open positions; increased understanding of the culture of the organization; and the political skills and key relationships required to advance.

What to look for in a mentor: A senior executive who is supportive of other key managers, well-respected in the company, gives others the opportunity to learn, and is known to be politically astute.

Officer-Level Mentoring

What do you need from a mentor? Information about what is really going on in the company, visibility at the top of the organization, and help with style issues that may be interfering with your success.

What to look for in a mentor: A senior executive who champions people, has the ear of the CEO, will be direct and honest, and manages an important strategic business area.

Top Executive-Level Mentoring

What do you need from a mentor? High-level support, good peer relationships, on the same wavelength as the CEO, and aware of your successes and accomplishments.

What to look for in a mentor: A senior decision maker close to the CEO and the mission of the organization who is approachable and has a history of supporting the careers of his or her key executives.

Just as you have different needs for mentoring at different times, there are a variety of types of mentors from which you can pick and choose. Here are some different "mentor types."

- A *formal mentor* is selected for you through a matching process by your company, usually by the human resources department. If there's not a formal program in your company, you can ask HR for help.
- A *top mentor* is a very senior executive in your company whom you want as your mentor. If you aim for the CEO or another top person to be your mentor, you'll need to plan your strategy carefully. His or her time is at a premium, and fewer and more informal meetings may work better.
- A *model mentor* is someone who has the traits you admire, and while you are carefully observing him or her and, in essence, using this person as a mentor—he or she doesn't know it. Each time you're in a meeting with the model mentor, you can gain additional insights.
- A *buddy mentor* is a peer or colleague with whom you have a "back and forth" relationship in assessing each other's skills or styles, helping each other informally. You should be familiar with each other's issues in order to be most helpful.
- An *invisible mentor* is an executive who supports you, monitors your progress, and ensures you are included in strategic initiatives. You are being mentored from afar, but may be unaware that he or she is taking an interest in your career. Since this is not uncommon, be alert to those around you and see if you have one!
- *Self-mentoring* doesn't involve a mentor relationship per se, but instead, you decide on the particular issues and challenges you'd like to improve and, through personal observation, gain insight from various people inside and outside your company with skills in those areas. Self-mentoring can be difficult and it takes an especially observant and self-motivated person to successfully mentor herself.
- A *reciprocal mentor* relationship has a two-way flow in which both people are acting as both mentor and mentee, each giving the other specific

knowledge and feedback in mentoring meetings. Reciprocal mentors both give and receive valuable advice and insights.

Tip: Tread Lightly to the Top

If you think the CEO is the best mentor for you, give careful thought on how to approach him or her. Ask for "advice from time to time" rather than actual mentoring. The CEO may feel more comfortable in a relationship that's less structured and more strategic. If he or she is tough to approach, try e-mailing about the progress of an important project you're working on, or a new idea you have, to initially get the CEO's attention. Follow up by sending something to his or her attention every quarter to establish a relationship.

It may be useful to have some or all of these different types of mentoring relationships at various times in your career. Dana's first experience with mentoring, though she didn't identify it as a form of "mentoring" at the time, was learning from a *model mentor*. Early in her career, she felt that she wasn't communicating effectively and noticed that one of her clients did a wonderful job in this area—when Mary Jane spoke, everyone listened. Dana was curious to find out what Mary Jane was doing to achieve this winning style. So, when she could, she sat in meetings Mary Jane was leading, watched her closely, and took notes on style, language, cadence—even the structure of her communication. Dana practiced using some of Mary Jane's techniques in speeches and meetings she ran. Her client never knew it, but Dana learned a great deal from her and now prides herself in her strong communication skills.

Becky realized she had an *invisible mentor*, an executive vice president of her company, when she was invited to his home—and it came as an eye-opener. He had interviewed her at the time she was hired as director of product development but she rarely saw him. When she walked into his holiday party, she couldn't help but notice that she was the only person there at her level (vice president)—all the others were higher level executives and people she considered personal friends of the host. She was both surprised and flattered. She thought back to when she was unexpectedly put on a strategic committee he ran and, another time, when he suggested she get to know the operations director he had just hired. When she put these pieces together, she realized that he had been supporting her behind the scenes and, in essence, helping others to know and value her. Though she had not directly approached him for advice, thinking he was too important to bother, he had been keeping an eye on her career—to her advantage.

The Roles of Mentor and Mentee

Taking on the role of either a *mentor* or *mentee* involves many challenges and responsibilities, as well as rewards. Being a *mentee* provides a unique opportunity to grow and learn from someone with greater and different experience than yours. You often forge a positive long-lasting relationship with your mentor. Here are some pointers to keep in mind for your role as a mentee.

Five Rules for a Mentee

1. Plan to call or visit your mentor at least every six weeks to keep the relationship fresh, unless the mentor is so senior that fewer meetings are appropriate.
2. Check in with her when one of her ideas or introductions has worked to tell her what happened.
3. Don't be concerned if your mentor doesn't embody *all* the styles and behaviors you are trying to improve. Take advantage of those she does offer!
4. If you see your mentor getting in trouble or sidelined in her career, be ready to rethink your strategy. Are you overly associated with her? Would it be wise to disengage?
5. Give permission for your mentor to be candid in giving you feedback on your style after a meeting, conference call, or interaction. Don't be defensive when you receive tough feedback!

On the other hand, being a *mentor* requires some guidelines too, as you'll see when you take on this role. In addition to giving of yourself, the experience will also help you review, learn, and improve your own skills. Effective leaders are known for mentoring others in their companies, so making time for this activity is essential.

Five Rules for a Mentor

1. Find the time for a mentoring relationship—the rewards are many.
2. Promote your mentee in meetings and discussions whenever possible.
3. Look for other colleagues whom your mentee may benefit from knowing and make appropriate introductions.
4. Understand your mentee's strengths. Watch for projects and initiatives that match her skills and interests, and nominate her for participation.
5. Help your mentee by selecting her most important areas for improvement and concentrate on those.

Finding Your Ideal Mentor

When looking for a mentor, think about the qualities that make a good mentor, assess and prioritize your needs, review the potential "candidates" available to you, and match your needs with them.

As you do the next exercises, keep in mind the *key qualities* for a mentor. Good mentors:

- give career advice and honest feedback;
- possess corporate insights and are knowledgeable about market information;
- have access to powerful people and can make introductions.

What are the areas where *you* can benefit from a mentoring relationship? Looking at the list below, rank the top five areas where you need help based on feedback you've received or areas in which you know you're weak. Rank the attribute you would be most interested in learning more about as number one.

Attributes	Ranking
Political savvy	—
Presence and style	—
Leadership	—
Communication skills	—
Power and influence	—
Negotiation skills	—
Sales ability	—
Career management	—
Functional expertise (finance, marketing, sales, etc.)	—
Company connections	—
Outside board connections	—
Industry specialist	—
Competitor knowledge	—

Now that you've ranked the areas where you can benefit from additional knowledge, list your top five below in order from one to five, and add the people you know who possess them. For example, if you ranked "leadership" as number one because it's highly important to you to gain insight on how to be a better leader and improve your own leadership skills, put it first on the list below. Then think of the people who embody the leadership qualities you seek. Your boss? A member of the executive team in your company? Write their names down in the spaces to the right.

Attribute:	Key People I Know Who Have This Attribute:
1. _____	_____
	_____
	_____
2. _____	_____
	_____
	_____
3. _____	_____
	_____
	_____
4. _____	_____
	_____
	_____
5. _____	_____
	_____
	_____

After reviewing these lists, you should have a better idea of *what it is you want and need* from a mentor, *who* on your list of possibilities meets your criteria, and who has the *key qualities* of a good mentor. Now you'll want to further fine-tune the possible candidates for the role. Based on all of the considerations we've discussed, list your top three possible mentor candidates.

My Mentor Candidates

1. _____

2. _____

3. _____

Tip: Don't Dis the Boss!

When making your list of possible company mentors—don't leave out your boss. If your company culture includes discussing mentoring with your manager and sharing a "wish list" of potentials, be sure to put him or her on your list. Your manager probably feels he or she has a substantial investment in you and your success—perhaps even hired you. Don't let the boss feel you don't value him or her as a mentor.

Take a look at the "mentor candidates" you have identified. Perhaps they're people you don't know yet, but have only heard about or observed. Think about who embodies the leadership qualities of the future in your organization. Then test out your possible candidates to see if they would make good mentors. For each candidate, ask yourself the following questions. If you don't know some of the answers, discreetly ask people who know or work for him or her.

Find Out about Your Possible Mentor

- Is the person approachable?
- Has he or she done mentoring before?
- Is this someone who would be honest with you?
- Does this person currently have a protégé or mentee?
- Does he or she have relationships with people at various organization levels?
- Is the person well-regarded in the company?
- Does he or she have the respect of the most powerful people in the company?
- Does he or she embody leadership and professionalism?
- Do the skills and experience of the person match your needs?
- Do you know this person, or know of someone who does?

You may have answered yes to many of the questions regarding one of your possible candidates. You'll probably want to review the candidate with your boss or human resources to get a second opinion. At the same time, you can go over your plan for how to approach this person. You should not be deterred from finding a way to go after a mentoring relationship, even if it requires laying some groundwork to connect with him or her.

Finding an Outside Mentor

What if you are unable to find a mentor inside your company? Perhaps you have looked for a mentor using the previous guidelines within your organization and have not found one. It could be that you want a woman mentor, and the candidate you've selected in your company is not available because she is overburdened with other mentees, or just too busy. The next step may be to look for a mentor outside your organization. There are several ways to tackle this:

- Think about who you've worked for and with at prior companies.
- Ask the mentor candidate in your company to suggest someone outside.
- Discuss the situation with your boss and ask for a referral.
- Ask a colleague at another company for a suggestion.
- Review possible candidates from the people you've met in your community work, professional associations, conferences, and other activities.

Once again, list the areas you've ranked from one to five, and add the people you know *outside your company* who possess them.

Have you found good potential mentors? List the three top mentor candidates from outside your company.

Tip: Former Bosses Make Great Mentors

A former boss from another company can be a great choice for a mentor. Chances are, if you've had a good relationship with him or her, this person has already provided you with either formal or informal mentoring at one time or another. You have a history together. She or he knows your work—along with your strengths and weaknesses. So, if you don't find a mentor inside your current company, approach a past boss and bring him or her up to date on your present job and employer, and the specific advice you need.

Attribute:	Key People I Know Who Have This Attribute:
1. _____	_____
	_____
	_____
2. _____	_____
	_____
	_____
3. _____	_____
	_____
	_____
4. _____	_____
	_____
	_____
5. _____	_____
	_____

My Mentor Candidates

1. _____
2. _____
3. _____

Male versus Female Mentors

You may decide, based on what you need and who is available, that it is desirable to have "multiple mentors." As an example, you might want to have a senior woman mentor who is valuable for what she can share with you about how she developed strategic relationships, and a man who has the ability to make things happen in your career with his powerful corporate connections. Each is valuable in his or her own way, and it may be to your benefit to take advantage of both. It is unrealistic to expect one person to have all the attributes you need and fulfill all roles.

As one woman surveyed commented, "I recommend you get both male and female mentors. Men and women are wired differently and have different points of view, and both are valuable." Since the executive suite is dominated by men, with only 8 percent of executive jobs in the top U.S. companies held by women, it is advisable—and practical—to have the perspective of a male mentor. In fact, there are circumstances when it might be your only option. Not surprisingly, 81 percent of the women we surveyed have been mentored by men.

While male mentors may in some cases have more clout or experience, there are exclusively female issues you'll want to discuss with a woman. For example, a male mentor probably won't be much help on subjects such as child care, balancing work and family, and style issues—and most women feel more comfortable talking with other women about these subjects anyway. And, when it comes to "bonding" on the obstacles and barriers women face in the corporate environment, it's definitely a woman-to-woman conversation.

If you are seeking a female mentor, you may have to enlarge your search to someone outside your organization. Connie Duckworth, a former investment banker and author, told *Fortune* magazine, "Every senior woman I know devotes an immense amount of time to mentoring. . . . they're mentoring every woman in the company." Indeed, if there are few senior women, and many women in the pipeline who need mentoring, it may be tough to get the attention of your ideal mentor. If there is a successful woman in your organization, however, it's worth trying to get a slice of her time for a particular area and then using one or two other mentors to supplement her expertise.

There is a danger, however, in taking on too many mentors. One or two at the same time is probably best. The reason for this is that it takes time to truly develop a meaningful mentoring relationship and if you have too many relationships, you are probably not reaping all the benefits from each one. Another possibility is that you can wind up getting conflicting advice from different mentors. These mixed signals can cause confusion, and end up being counterproductive to your efforts.

Whomever you choose, you'll want your mentor to be a straight shooter who gives you candid advice and counsel—even if it's not what you want to hear. Without this trait, he or she is not helping you, and may even be doing you a disservice. A vice president in a leading financial institution, Gale had been working with a mentor with whom she had a good relationship, though he did not always tell her what she wanted to hear. In fact, he was sometimes brutally honest. They were both attending a meeting one afternoon when the discussion heated up between Gale and a colleague and resulted in a public argument. Afterward, her mentor took her aside and told her she was out of line and shouldn't have let the disagreement accelerate. She was stung that he was criticizing her, and started to defend her actions by saying her colleague had been in the wrong. Her mentor said, "You're right, Gale, he *was* wrong. But you were wrong to deal with it that way. You're going to have to carry that baggage around now, and you don't need extra baggage." He was very firm—and very direct! After listening, Gale realized that even though she was initially hurt, he was right and the message he gave her was important: *don't fight battles at the expense of winning the war, especially in a public setting.*

How to Approach a Possible Mentor

So, now that you have identified your potential mentor candidate(s), how do you approach them? There are a number of ways to do this.

- The *direct way* is to speak to him or her in an informal setting or make an appointment. Let that person know that you would like to seek advice on a particular subject and ask if that would be agreeable. If you already know the person, it is easier to do this—if not, it's a bit harder. Be strong, and after a meeting where you're together, walk up and introduce yourself.
- If you don't know the person, have little chance of crossing paths, or are uncertain about approaching him or her, you can *indirectly* make contact through someone else. If you know someone who can make the introduction, that is a good option. You can also ask human resources to help you. If you don't have a contact or feel comfortable going to HR, call your potential mentor's office to make an appointment. If asked about the purpose of the meeting, just be honest and say that it is to discuss your career and possible mentoring.
- A third option is to *ask your boss or manager* to make an introduction to a potential mentor. You can do this during a performance review in which you and your manager are discussing areas where you can improve your performance, knowledge, or style, but it can just as easily be a separate follow-up discussion.

Having the actual conversation can be tricky, so here are some examples to work from. When you are ready to approach your mentor, it will help to draft an opening statement. For example, if you decided you needed advice on how to manage your career, you could say something like this:

> **Career Advice Opening Statement**: Thank you so much for meeting with me. I have been at the company for five years and feel I'm ready to acquire additional skills and experience. I've observed and admired your work and career, and as I look at my own goals and objectives, I'd consider it valuable to be able to learn from some of your experience. Would you consider serving as my mentor and giving me advice on how to manage my career?

Or, let's imagine you need insights from someone who has experience in a specific area. You might link your request to the human resources process and say:

> **Work/Life Balance Opening Statement**: I appreciate your giving me some time. I love my job and am committed to my career. During the last few years, my life has changed because I've had two children and I've encountered many new issues with work and family. At my annual review, it was suggested I work with a mentor. I know from our conversations that you are married with three children. I would be very interested to hear how you have balanced family and work and to be able to talk with you about some of these issues from time to time.

Perhaps you want guidance on your style because you've been told it's an area in which you can improve. You might say:

> **Communication Style Opening Statement**: Thank you for taking the time to meet with me today. I'm excited about the work I've been doing with my team. I've noticed, however, that when I lead meetings I often have trouble getting and keeping the attention of the group and I've received feedback that I need to fine-tune my style of communication. I've watched your ability to command an audience and deliver your message effectively—and would like to understand how you developed this talent and get your feedback on my style. Could

we meet to discuss the areas I need to improve and your suggestions
for me?

These are merely guidelines and you'll want to adapt the language to your
own situation and your personal style.

If this is your first foray into mentoring, start by selecting one candidate
from your list of inside or outside mentors, define what you want from the
relationship, develop a strategy for contacting him or her, and draft an opening statement. Now you're ready to approach your mentor candidate.

Approaching My Mentor Candidate

Mentor Candidate:

What I Want:

Strategy for Contact:

Opening Statement:

How Your Company Can Help You

As we mentioned, you may find that your organization can help you in
establishing mentor relationships. In a 2003 survey in which we interviewed
executives from Fortune 1000 companies, mentoring was available at all
companies in one form or another. Some of the programs available include:

- Formal one-on-one mentoring in which human resources typically
  matches mentor and mentee
- Informal mentoring relationships initiated by an employee seeking a
  mentor, or a manager/executive who sees potential in an employee

- Mentoring circles consisting of senior management mentors working with a group of up to ten people
- Affinity groups such as a women's network established to advise and train women leaders

Formal mentoring programs usually include the company identifying high-potential women candidates and pairing these women with appropriate senior executives, either male or female. In some cases, they are specifically paired with a mentor who is in a section of the business that is different from their own. Other companies use a structure in which the president and each of his or her direct reports mentor a high-potential woman. One high-level woman at a global company said it this way: "Women need senior-level mentors. It has to be the right chemistry between them so they can share their dreams and their mentor can help make them come true. My company did that for me when I was in middle management."

While there are formal programs in which mentor and mentee are trained in the mentoring process and develop goals that are monitored periodically by human resources, informal programs range from having mentoring be at the discretion of departments and individuals, to programs that encourage people to get together on their own. Though these are not tracked by human resources, in some cases educational sessions are given on mentoring as well as other tools such as videos and handouts.

If your company does not have a formal mentoring process or women's program, take the initiative and start one. You can assert and define your leadership in the organization through taking the lead on establishing a women's mentoring network or affinity group. If you choose to initiate a women's program within your company, here are steps to create a successful program.

Step #1: Build the Business Case

Answer the question "why do we need this?" by scanning the environment for what other companies are doing and, importantly, *reaping* from their programs. Create an urgency about the value of a women's initiative by promoting the benefits to the women as well as the company. These include:

- Increased retention and recruitment of talented women
- Decreased cost from losing talented people who get frustrated by the culture

- A talent pool for success, as well as greater innovation, diversity, and creativity of thought

Step #2: Enlist Support from the Top Down

Enlist all the support you can get from the top and on down the line, starting with the CEO and continuing with senior management and human resources. If possible, identify a senior executive sponsor to lead the initiative. He or she can help to plan, design, and launch the program.

Step #3: Get the Vision Right

Once you have a guiding team in place, develop a vision and strategy that will work for your company. Consult with the senior women in the organization to get their views and support. Identify and link with the mission of the organization and its diversity goals, as well as already existing organizational support programs.

Step #4: Plan Steps and Launch

Create a plan. Identify key issues for participants through focus groups and employee surveys, and design programs to meet their needs. Develop a communications strategy. Flesh out follow-up support. Then, launch the program and gain traction through publicizing and promoting each effort through the company newsletter, internal website, and any other available means.

Step #5: Measure Outcomes

Establish a benchmark of your progress compared to other companies like yours, and evaluate and measure results. Your objective, if possible, is to establish an economic value that the company can measure over time. Key measurements include expense savings, brand awareness, company name recognition, and market share.

Once you've gotten your program off the ground, don't let up. Keep pushing forward, tweaking to make it better, and establishing "wins." You'll know it has succeeded when it becomes an integral part of the corporate culture—and it's a flat-out home run if the CEO mentions it in his letter in the annual report!

Tip: Invite the Men!

If you're starting a mentoring program, engage key men in your company in the women's initiative. Invite them to join the planning and kickoff meetings. Men who are supportive of the idea will bring ideas to the meetings and, even better, will talk it up with their buddies and help you spread the word. They are important to the effort and can be strong allies. If excluded, they may resent it.

The Pitfalls of Mentoring

While the benefits of mentoring are many and varied, there are some potential pitfalls to be avoided. For example, you can find yourself:

Overshadowed. If you are seen as "under the wing" of one person, you may find that colleagues and superiors don't attribute results directly to you. Instead, they may think that your work is heavily influenced by your mentor, which can limit your possibilities and promotions. There may even be resentment and the feeling that you'd be a nonachiever without your mentor.

Dependent. Relying too much on a mentor can cause you to be indecisive and even insecure. If you feel you have to get your mentor's input on every move, it may be that you need to individuate and move on in order to grow and develop independently.

Vulnerable. If you've hitched your wagon to one star, and your mentor gets into trouble politically or leaves the organization under negative circumstances, you may find that it spills over to you. If you're directly connected to just one person, you may suffer the same fate as he or she does.

A number of years back, the president of a management consulting firm hired Allicia as a consultant. The president was a well-connected and highly regarded woman in the community, and the chemistry was great. She was clearly eager to act as a mentor to Allicia, so as time went on, she included her in a number of activities including strategy sessions and meetings with community leaders. Allicia was getting the experience of a lifetime and learning more than she dreamed possible. People had come to expect her to attend the important meetings that her boss was a part of, and she was considered her "protégée." Eventually, as Allicia grew in her career there, she began to feel confined in her role. There was no chance for promotion because there wasn't a position to move to. Her boss was the star and rainmaker of the company, and Allicia realized she would be in her shadow for as long as she stayed. It was a very tough decision, but she knew she had to move on. Her mentor was sorely disappointed when Allicia had this very difficult discussion with her, but eventually she understood. It was the right decision for Allicia, and to this day, she learns from her former boss and considers her to be a strong champion and close friend.

Tip: Know When It's Over

When you know in your gut that you've received all possible benefit from a mentoring relationship, it's time to move on. Depending on your past connection, you might consider your former mentor a good future friend. If that isn't viable, have a discussion reviewing the relationship and all it's done for you and your career, thank him or her, and end the formal relationship. Keep the door open by asking for the okay to come back and talk in the future.

Sally, who is now head of a large market research firm, had a mentoring relationship early in her career that lasted fourteen years—longer than her marriage! Her mentor, a man, was a couple of rungs higher than she was on the corporate ladder. When the relationship began, she was at the beginning of her career and her mentor was extremely valuable to her in a number of ways: he understood corporate politics, was technically knowledgeable, and was able to relay important information. As they both moved up in the organization, people began, more and more, to link them and their work together.

As time went on, Sally began to feel that she was always in his shadow and not perceived as an independent person who was talented in her own right. She also detected resentment from colleagues who felt that she received special treatment because she and her mentor were so close. She ignored the signals for a long time until she finally acknowledged the problem and made a pivotal decision. In order to continue her personal and career growth, she knew she would have to separate from him. After all those years, she looked for and found a new job in a different company, where she excelled on her own.

Mentorship vs. Sponsorship

As we have discussed in this chapter, mentors can be formal or informal, and provide advice and feedback on various aspects of leadership behavior, career success strategies, and organizational politics. A "sponsor" is someone in a pivotal role in an organization who takes a more direct role in your career. Though not a coach, a sponsor's goal is to get you ahead in your career, for reasons which can vary.

A sponsor is a senior executive who sees real potential in you and has identified you as a good fit for the organization and its future. He or she is likely to be impressed with your capabilities and believes that you fit into his or her succession planning for the company. A sponsor takes ownership of your career trajectory, often working behind the scenes on an executive committee and/or with human resources as they develop a leadership plan for the future of the organization.

If you know that you have a sponsor, consider yourself fortunate! If you are not sure, open your eyes to the possibility. In any case, making yourself visible—in a positive way—within the organization will position you for this possibility. By the time women reach the senior ranks, many have received the mentoring they need. Now it's time to find a sponsor!

Why Women Must Mentor—and Sponsor

Mentoring is a must, though it requires time most women don't feel they have. It is vital for senior women to help other women as mentors in order to build up the numbers of women in corporate America. Women need to have women mentors they can turn to for advice, counsel, and encouragement—and who can provide a critical connection within their organizations. This "connectedness" is an important element in the retention of women executives in corporations. In order to build the critical mass of women needed at or near the top to begin to impact the culture of companies, women who have made it, or who are higher on the organization chart, must make an effort to lend a hand to others in the form of mentorship or, as possible, sponsorship.

One way to share your experiences with other women without taking on too many mentees is to say yes when you're asked to speak to women's groups in your community. The connections you make through meeting people in this setting are positive in many ways. It gives you a boost to know that you're enriching your audience, while it helps improve your speaking and listening skills. Speaking to a group is not the same as one-on-one mentoring, yet it's a good way to touch your audience and pass on information and experience.

Mentoring women is also a means to inspire other women through your success, knowledge, and wisdom. If you've made it to a top position, it's hard to avoid being viewed as a role model by others. Take it for what it is—a great compliment. And though it may initially make you a bit uneasy, give it time and you'll become comfortable in this role.

CHAPTER 6

Maintain Your Balance
Take Control of Your Work and Life

THE ALARM goes off at 6:00 a.m. and you're off and running. Shower, makeup, hair, grabbing the "next in line" outfit in the closet. You peek into your son's room to make sure he's up and getting ready. You feed the cat, glance at your schedule for the day, and scan the paper in order to stay current. When your son comes down, you make him breakfast and while he's eating, check his homework and inquire about his science project. You have a brief conversation about the day's schedule and when Dad is coming back from his business trip. You quickly put the dishes in the sink, load your two briefcases into the car, and hurry your son along so you can drive him to school. He's at school by 7:30, and you check voice mail on the way to your 8:00 a.m. breakfast meeting. No time for a workout today.

After breakfast, you return three calls on the way to the office, find yourself in a traffic jam, and arrive just in time for a 9:30 meeting with your boss to review progress on the strategic guidelines you're writing for the department. Afterward, you check e-mail, respond to the urgent ones, return phone calls, and talk with one of your employees about a deadline for a report. At 11:30, you quickly check hair and makeup in your compact mirror—no time for the ladies' room—and you're off to network at a luncheon meeting of your professional association. After lunch, it's back to the office in time for a

2:00 p.m. meeting with an outside vendor to negotiate pricing on a product he's selling. Explaining that you have to leave early for another commitment, you agree that everything can be covered in an hour, which you do by getting right down to business.

You coordinate a number of items with your assistant and after hurriedly packing up your papers and checking messages once again, you leave for a board meeting of a nonprofit organization. The meeting is to run from 4:00 to 6:00, but you tell the chairman that you'll need to duck out by 5:00 today. Your son's soccer game began at 4:00, and you catch his eye as you arrive late in the third quarter.

Following the game, you and your son go home for dinner and you try to explain to him why you missed his goal in the first quarter. You clean up after dinner, tidy the house, and throw a load of laundry in the wash as you catch up on the TV news. You've scheduled a quick call at 8:00 p.m. with a woman you're mentoring which lasts half an hour. Then, you start to review a report which had been left on your desk. A final conversation with your son, a glance around the house for anything that needs care, a hunt to find a pair of shoes for tomorrow, one last look at your e-mail, and, exhausted, you go to bed.

Tomorrow, it starts all over again . . .

Being a woman today is a major balancing act. We are organizers, nurturers, planners, and caregivers as well as bread-winners, thinkers, and doers. We are also bosses, employees, friends, wives, mothers, sisters, and daughters. We are remarkably multifaceted and because we have these responsibilities all day, every day, we are faced with tremendous conflicts. According to Catalyst, nearly two-thirds of female executives have children, so there are many of us working full-time and trying to succeed at managing it all, each with different stories and varying degrees of success.

It is not surprising that women feel more overworked than men—because most often they are. The Leader's Edge research confirmed in a 2002 study that, unlike men, *most executive women who work full-time also are responsible for traditional household chores and child care in addition to their day-to-day corporate responsibilities.* As they advance in the corporate world, women rely more on outside support for chores and child care, but continue to bear most of the responsibility for cleaning, meal preparation, and child-care arrangements. In essence, we work all day and go home to a second job. No wonder we find it difficult to maintain a work/life balance.

Tip: Is Doing It All Doing You In?

If your schedule and responsibilities are veering out of control, ask yourself what tasks can be delegated or rearranged to free up more time. How about hiring a cleaning service or sending the laundry out? Does your family really need a homemade meal—or can it be take out? Is your out-of-the-way hairdresser worth the extra thirty minutes? Wherever you can, try to make things more streamlined by changing the way you do something, letting it go, or hiring someone else to do it.

Even more so than male colleagues, women consider work/life balance the key to their quality of life. There isn't a woman I meet with who doesn't have the issue of "How do I do it all?" One senior executive said, "I wanted some balance in my life. I worked eight to eight and beyond. I never stopped working or thinking about work—including on weekends. I finally realized I had to discover what made me happy, not what made the company happy." The women executives surveyed by The Leader's Edge expressed a strong need for a more balanced life with more flexible working hours. In fact, it was a major factor in why women left their jobs, frequently moving to companies that would accommodate their needs for flexibility or starting their own businesses. Only a small number chose to leave the workforce entirely.

In Anna's case, a life change required rethinking her work environment. A senior associate with a law firm on the fast track to partner, Anna returned to her job at the end of her six-week maternity leave. When she left work each night at 6:00 p.m., she noticed that her colleagues seemed to be watching her, and she recognized that it was because most of them left closer to 8:00 p.m. They were wondering why she was leaving so early by their standards, and how she got away with it. Even though she billed the same number of hours that they did by working efficiently, she soon realized that the firm's perception was her reality. Their standards for partner were no longer compatible with her life, and the firm's culture would never change. Knowing she was no longer on track for partner, she decided that staying would only lead to increased frustration and that she needed to make a change. She found a position as associate dean at a law school that fit her skills, her need to leave work at a reasonable hour, and her new family situation.

Janet didn't go to a different organization—she started her own. An admitted workaholic, she routinely put in twelve-hour days at her job. She was vice president of marketing for an industrial products company at which long hours were expected without consideration of the personal lives of the employees. Janet was married, had no children, and because her husband was in a position where he traveled a great deal, she embraced the demands of her job. Eventually, her husband started a new job and was able to spend more time at home. Janet began to reconsider her lifestyle. She was constantly stressed by her desire to spend time with him and she also realized she didn't have any time for friends, reading, hobbies, or relaxation. Her schedule lacked balance and she felt that she needed a more well-rounded life. After a particularly tough time at work, she made the decision to leave and start her own marketing firm that, as difficult as it was to get off the ground, allowed her to control her own schedule and call the shots.

There is clearly no right answer on how to create a work/life balance. It depends on your individual circumstances, employer's policies, and capacity for making it all work. The fact is that not everyone can, or has the desire to, try to "do it all." Many working women want to add more facets to their lives, but aren't sure they can make it work. Some have tried a path, decided for one reason or another it wasn't working well, and changed courses.

Biology and sociology have put women in the unique situation of having life choices that do not apply to men. These choices can actually make it more difficult for women, because they present us with many possible directions and no one "right" answer. While one woman can balance a senior-level position, husband, and three children—with time for friends and outside activities—another will feel that the best course is to take a sabbatical when she has children. Still another choice is the decision not to have children at all in order to succeed at work, or the opposite—to stay home and raise children at the expense of a career.

The smaller choices, as well as the big ones, can cause confusion and disappointment, no matter what you do. If you choose a networking meeting over a workout with a friend, you may feel guilty about not meeting your friend's expectations and frustration that you didn't keep up with your fitness plan. On the other hand, you made an important contact at your meeting and were seen at a high-level function. It seems like we're always coming up against someone else's—even our own—expectations because we'd like to please everyone.

Making the Right Choice for You

To help you think through your options and choices for work/life balance, answer the following questions, which are divided into categories.

Depending on your stage of life and goals, some categories may be more relevant than others. The idea here is to help stimulate your thinking and help you gain perspective on where you are in balancing your life, where you want to be, and what's best for you. If you discover areas where you have issues, it may be wise to seek the advice you need to solve your individual challenges.

Category: Work/Life

How you feel about your work will have a substantial impact on your attitude and commitment to balancing all of your responsibilities.

Do I feel good about my career path? Many people end up moving into jobs that don't really match their skills and interests. If you find you're no longer satisfied with where your career is going, it may be a good time to reevaluate your situation and consider making a change. Don't confuse job satisfaction with the larger issue of work/life balance or you risk making a rash decision to leave the workforce. Matching your job with your skills and abilities will provide much more satisfaction and ultimate success, and permit you to evaluate your life goals more objectively.

Am I advancing in my career? Have you gone for two years or more without a promotion? If so, it's time to have a conversation with your boss about your future. If you feel your career is stagnating, it will affect your attitude and decision making. If you've been passed over for promotions or openings in your company, it's time to get real feedback on why and how you are perceived by your boss and others.

How supportive of my career is my boss? Does your boss support you? Are you getting opportunities to grow? Are you considered for, and given, special projects and initiatives? If not, you may be stuck with a boss who's not going to be much help in furthering your career. Even if you have a good working relationship, your boss may not see it as in his or her best interests to promote you. If you sense that your boss is not committed to you and your career growth, you may want to think about how it will affect your future.

How much flexibility is there in my position? Do you find that your boss eyes the clock when you leave for the day? Are your hours scrutinized— instead of the work you produce? If you've noticed that there are no other women who have flexibility in their working arrangements, it may indicate that there are limited options in your company. In this case, you will have to decide whether to confront the issue head-on, deal with it, or leave.

Do I have time for other activities in my life? Have you given up the things that you love to do—hobbies, fitness, cultural activities, spending time with friends and family? If your world is limited to work only, you will begin to feel isolated and resentful. There is a direct correlation between good health and physical fitness, a well-rounded life, and strong emotional relationships. You'll need to make some adjustments to your priorities or risk the emotional and physical consequences.

If you feel positive about your work, you're more likely to want to continue your career and have the ability to keep things in perspective. A woman who finally left an executive position she had grown to dislike told us, "I'm now doing something that is my own and I'm having fun. I still work long hours, but it doesn't feel like work. Those hours are in my control and I set a more flexible schedule. No more long meetings without a real purpose!" Her former company was not meeting her needs and though she probably puts the same amount of time into her new position, she's enjoying it and feeling less stress.

If you have matched your skills and strengths to your work, you'll be happier and more successful. If you're unhappy, it may signal an ideal time for you to reassess your interests. (See chapter 8, "Keep Your Career on Track.")

Tip: Dare to Change

Be honest in your assessment of your situation and don't be afraid to consider changing jobs, career, or other aspects of your life. Be open to change, consider your options, and give yourself time to envision how things could be different, and possibly better. Always get advice and information from others you trust before you leap.

Category: Personality

The type of personality you have is important in determining how you are able to handle the many facets of your life.

Do I have issues with perfection and control? Do you feel that everyone and everything must be up to your high standards of perfection? If you see something you consider amiss, do you have a compulsion to step in and redo it? Do you have the need to control your home and work environments? These are traits that will cause major anxiety and bog you down. Try to focus on what's important and let the other things go.

Do I have enough energy? Stress can sap you of energy. Are you irritable and unfocused because you're not sleeping well? If you're constantly tired, look at what you are and are not doing on a daily basis that causes you to feel this way. Study your schedule, try to get enough sleep, and make more time for yourself.

How do I handle stress? Do you take your stress out on your friends and family? Do you pop aspirin for the headaches you get every day? Do you feel trapped or oppressed by your situation? Do you think you've made too many compromises? Recognize what is causing your behavior, get to the root of the problem, and address it by making necessary changes. Don't be afraid to seek the help of a professional to give you an outsider's perspective on your life.

Do I feel I'm trying to do too much? Are you always on the run? Do you have trouble saying no to requests—even those you don't have time for? Recognize that you're on a treadmill, and spend the time to assess how you can take some pressure off. Learn how to be more assertive so you can say no, or you may find yourself always holding the bag.

Am I too tightly wound? Do you feel like you never get things wrapped up at the end of a week? Are you lacking time to think about where you've been and where you're going? If you're racing from morning till night, you will find yourself constantly reacting to events. Instead, put two hours a week on your calendar to reflect and plan—you'll become calmer and more effective.

Personality traits can work for or against you as your life becomes increasingly complex. A perfectionist, for example, is in danger of burning out because she is used to being highly organized, detail-oriented, and in control of everything in her life. An executive at a search firm with two small children swears that ten years ago, her need for control was so strong that she would have fallen apart on what is now a typical day for her. Today, while she still considers herself a very organized person, her house doesn't have to be spotless and she's learned to be more flexible and accepting of circumstances beyond her control.

Another woman, an analyst with a lobbying organization, feels her perfectionist personality probably contributed to her inability to manage work and home. She was unwilling, or unable, to change and couldn't bring herself to leave work until her projects were "perfect." That equaled very long hours away from home. She ended up having to choose between job and home, and she chose home. These are two very bright and competent women, each with an admitted need to control. One made some changes to her style and stayed in her high-powered career. The other opted not to change and made the only decision that worked for her.

Tip: **Stop Sweating the Small Stuff**

*What are the things that make **you** sweat? How about running late for a meeting or appointment, thinking about a comment made to you by someone in the office, worrying about something you said or did, agonizing because you didn't get to the cleaners or missed someone's birthday? You can't change it or control it—so accept it instead. Acknowledge that something has occurred that has annoyed or disappointed you and, if there's corrective action, take it. If not, tell yourself to put it aside and move on. Repeat after me: "accept."*

Category: Children

When you have children, your responsibilities increase dramatically, which makes it doubly a challenge to strike a balance between work and home life.

Do I feel that I spend enough time with my children? Every child wants more time with his or her mother—so you may never feel that you are satisfying your child. The quality, rather than the amount, of time spent is the key issue. If your children are young, do you play together and read to them when you get home? If they're older, do you take the time to talk with them—and to listen? Can they always reach you on your cell phone? Do they know they are your top priority even though you work? These are truly the important things.

Does my spouse or partner participate in the child care? Do you encourage your spouse to spend time with the kids—or do you actually discourage him by acting as though there's only one right way to do things (your way)? Let go a little and encourage him to get involved, even if he doesn't do it quite up to your standards. Give him time with the kids without planning it for him. Parity in child care is essential.

Are my current child-care arrangements satisfactory? The stress of not being confident in your child care can be tremendous. Try to be certain, in your own mind, that you are totally comfortable with whatever arrangement you choose, or you may not be able to devote yourself to anything else. Make a change immediately if you feel your child-care arrangement is not working or is not safe. Ask other working mothers about their solutions.

Do I spend enough time with my spouse or significant other? Have you let your children, your job, and running the household get in the way of your relationship? Make enough time to keep your relationship the best it can be—it's the core of your happiness. Children make this one of the trickiest issues for couples. Carving out a standing weekly "just the two of us night" could be the answer.

An officer of a bank, Barbara amazed all her work colleagues as well as her boss when, after having a child, she returned to work a month later. She was very detail-oriented and had planned everything ahead of time. She knew that getting back to work was vital to her well-being, even though it meant sacrificing much of her free time and temporarily putting aside a couple of hobbies. She was delighted in the time she spent with her daughter, but knew that she truly enjoyed her work, and she and her husband loved having two incomes. She couldn't imagine stopping work, even for a period of time. Because she was determined, organized, and engaged with her work, she could handle the situation when, a few years later, she and her husband divorced. Her career continued with multiple promotions and her daughter, as she grew up, noted and respected her mom's achievements. Barbara has always felt she kept her balance, and her identity.

Another woman, a nursing supervisor at a major hospital, was unsure of her plans for the future when she left her position to have a baby. About four months later, she was back full-time. When asked if it was tough leaving the baby in the morning, she smiled and said, "Actually, no. It works best for me and it's great for the baby. I have my 'adult' time at work, she has her 'social' time at day care, and we have our evenings to enjoy together."

There are also a number of important balance issues to consider when you're thinking about having a child.

What is my child-rearing philosophy? If you decide it's important for a parent to be home for a time, plan ahead so you stay engaged and current in your work, and don't lose your skills. You can study, do consulting, attend conferences, and generally stay tuned in to your industry. If you plan on working, be realistic about how you will handle child rearing and discuss it in advance with your spouse.

What kind of child-care arrangement would I like to have? If you plan on using a day-care center, research options convenient to home or work— perhaps your company offers day care. If you want to have someone come to your home, ask around and look at placement firms, international au-pair programs, and other options. Get recommendations from friends and neighbors—then decide for yourself what feels most comfortable.

Am I (and is my spouse) realistic about the sacrifices that may be required? Have you and your spouse discussed how you will balance work and family? Is he willing and able to share the burden? Try to talk through it and envision how it will work in your relationship and circumstances. Planning this major life event together will make a terrific difference. Your ideas may change as reality sets in, but this should be a partnership all the way.

How will a child, and child care, impact your finances? Ask yourself how much child care will cost, and analyze what that means to the family income and your style of living. It may end up that the costs for your child, including child care, will take up one of your salaries. It's something you need to know and plan for so there is no "blame game" later.

Face it: your childbearing years can be filled with the most guilt and conflict. There are numerous decisions to be made, and it is difficult to project how smoothly things will work out and how you will handle this huge life change. As important as it is to plan your career, it's impossible to plan your feelings. You can't plan how you'll feel when your child is born, the way a life change will play out day to day, and how that will affect your outlook. Even the best plans may need to be reassessed.

The strength of your support system will be a determining factor in many of your decisions. The more support you have, the more "under control" you will feel. Knowing that family, friends, and neighbors are available when there is the need can make all the difference in your ability to deal with things. It's part of an equation to keep in mind as you think about how—and if—you can put it all together. The formula consists of three elements: *a solid support system, quality child care, and an understanding employer.* Without these elements, it's hard to "do it all" and make it work.

Is Your Life in Balance?

If you're confused about your priorities, the next exercise will help you ascertain what's important. In this exercise, the objective is to determine how you are currently spending your time and whether you are doing the things that are important to you in life. Depending on your answers, you may want to commit to taking steps to put your priorities in more balance.

First, what are the five things that are most important to you in your life? The following list gives you some ideas on the types of things to think about.

Family	Career	Parents
Children	Travel	Leisure Activities
Spouse	Education	Physical Activities
Friends	Community Work	Money
Hobbies	Retirement	Spirituality

Once you've made your list of five, write down what you are currently doing in each of these areas, to see if you are spending time doing what you consider important. Depending on your answers, you may want to make a commitment to change what you're doing or the amount of time you're spending in a particular activity.

My Five Priorities: Examples

Example 1: Travel (I love to travel and experience new cities and cultures)
What I am currently doing: I didn't take all of my vacation time last year and don't have anything planned. I'll lose the vacation time I don't take. I haven't traveled to any of my favorite cities in years.

What I am going to change: I'm going to call the travel agent and plan the trip to Rome I've been thinking about. I need the getaway and I'm not setting a good example for my people if I don't go. I will schedule and take my vacation time every year from now on!

Example 2: My parents (they're getting older and won't be around forever!)
What I am currently doing: I'm frequently short with my mother when she calls me on Sundays and I only see my parents twice a year at holiday time.

What I am going to change: I'm going to make plans to see my parents more often—at least four times a year—so I can enjoy them and listen to their stories. If I plan a non-holiday visit, without my siblings there, I'll be able to spend more quality time with them, which will make me feel good.

Make *your* list on the next page!

Eight Barriers to Achieving Balance

Whatever the particulars of *your* hectic life, there are some clear "don'ts" when you're struggling to manage work, family, and the rest of your life— and maintain a modicum of sanity. Following is a list of the eight ways to make yourself miserable—*don't fall into the trap of these common mistakes.*

Feeling (Constantly) Guilty. When you're at work, you find yourself feeling guilty about not being at home—and when you're home, you're obsessed with that meeting you're missing. You cannot be in two (or three, or four) places at one time, and you need to give all your energy to your present undertaking. Let the guilt go—at least some of it!

Playing the Good Girl. So many of us have been taught to be considerate of others to a fault—even if it means saying yes when we should be say-

My Five Priorities

What I am currently doing:

What I am going to change:

What I am currently doing:

What I am going to change:

What I am currently doing:

What I am going to change:

What I am currently doing:

What I am going to change:

What I am currently doing:

What I am going to change:

Have you just made some commitments to change? If so, you're taking more control over your destiny, and by making these commitments, you will add to your life balance and make yourself feel better. It may help to put the five things you're going to change on a piece of paper and stick it on your mirror or bulletin board to remind yourself what is important to you.

ing no or waiting instead of speaking out. If you don't express your needs and get your voice heard, after a while your frustration level will reach the "bubbling-over" point. It's going to come out in the wrong place at the wrong time. Be confident enough to express yourself when you feel the need.

Second-Guessing Your Life. Just because you're having a bad day doesn't mean that you've made poor choices, or should question your whole life. Sometimes when you're in the midst of a crisis, you're tempted to make decisions too quickly. At these times, it's easy to start believing your neighbor's propaganda about working mothers, or your sister's criticism of your lifestyle. Don't allow yourself to fall into that trap. Correct or deal with the problem of the moment and move on, confidently. Rely on your instincts to know what's right for you.

Seeking Perfection. Whether it's appearance, performance on the job, running a household, or running a marathon, many of us are always trying to be "perfect" at whatever we're doing. The problem is—there's no such thing! Nobody can be a "10"; it just doesn't exist. Trying to attain perfection is unrealistic and unrewarding. Aiming for more realistic goals will keep you a lot happier and more productive—and it's likely your "less than perfect" will be better than most.

Neglecting "You." When time or energy runs out, the first thing to slip is usually—you. Although it's easier to cancel some of your activities (that hair appointment, time at the gym, or your book club) than to disappoint the boss, family, or friends, this won't work on a long-term basis. If you don't take enough time for you, you'll begin to wear down and wear out. Make yourself the priority, and do what is necessary to look and feel good in order to maintain balance and tackle the "nondiscretionary" tasks.

Saying Yes (When You Should Say No). Your child's teacher has asked you to chaperone a class trip. Or perhaps your boss requested that you fill in at a last-minute client meeting. Maybe your friend has invited you to a mid-week birthday celebration. How can you say no? Or, rather, can you say yes and maintain your equilibrium? Developing realistic priorities and being honest about them with others is the key to staying on course. Otherwise, you'll be creating additional stress and anxiety in your already complex life.

Going It Alone. As a highly capable person, it's natural to think, "I can handle it myself." After all, independence is a highly valued trait—and one that has gotten you far. But there are times when asking for help is both necessary and appropriate. In both your personal and business life, knowing when to ask for help can truly be a lifesaver when the "to do" list starts to become unmanageable.

Allowing Your Foundation to Crack. Though you have many facets to your life, at the core of it all is your family. Being clear about what's essential, setting aside time for your most important relationships, and developing boundaries to protect your family time are key elements to being happy. Without these, cracks will begin to surface in the foundation of your life and affect everything around you.

Doing What Works for You

Many women who work part-time say that the days they go to work are less stressful than their stay-at-home days. Janny, a part-timer, finds that her "home job" is more physically and mentally exhausting than her "career job." She says that a day with her children, though gratifying, leaves her brain feeling like "mush," but that she finds work stimulating.

There are many reasons why you might want to change from working full-time to part-time. These include spending more time with your children, going to graduate school, caring for an ailing parent, or giving yourself a break. In most cases, the shift to part-time work will be for a defined period of time. If you are a valued and valuable employee, chances are your company, regardless of precedent, will listen to your proposal.

Just as the reasons are varied, so are the possibilities on how to structure your work. You could:

- Share a job with someone else whose circumstances are such that they too would like to work part of the time;
- Redefine your present job to fit a part-time schedule and delegate specific duties to others;
- Take on a company project for your part-time work and ask for your present job to be filled by someone else.

There are also a number of alternatives regarding what "part-time" really means. Do you want to reduce your hours per day—or your number of days per week?

Maura was clever when she shaped her part-time hours. She'd been around long enough to know when her boss usually needed her, and when most of the critical department meetings occurred. With this in mind, she decided that in order to maintain her momentum while she worked part-time, she needed to be at the office every day. She works from nine to three, Monday through Friday, and finds that people are so accustomed to her hours that they barely miss her when she is off. Because she is doing so well in managing her department, she has actually been told that her "flex" work schedule is a nonissue in her career.

If you're planning to ask to work part-time, know what you want before you have a formal conversation with your boss. In preparation for this conversation, do your homework:

- Talk to other women who've gone part-time to gain their insight.
- Review the company's policy manual to see what their philosophy is on part-time.
- Structure a one-page proposal that will work for everyone—you, your boss, and the organization.

Then go to your boss with your proposal. Include the reason you're requesting a change, the specifics of what you're suggesting, how it fits into the company mission, and *what the benefits are to the company.*

There are many possible benefits, including the fact that your skills and experience are being retained at a lower cost, you have a desire to stay engaged with the company, and it's expensive to lose you. It will actually cost the company at least 150 percent of your salary to replace you, including replacement hiring, training, and lost productivity! Be organized, direct, and confident when you have this conversation. Keep in mind that if the company is reasonable, they will understand the value in what you're recommending. Once you've made your case, leave your plan on paper behind so that your boss—who may initially be surprised—will have the specifics in front of him or her. Tell your boss you'll check back in a day or two to get his or her thoughts and to decide on the next steps. By following this procedure, you've given yourself every chance of success in gaining acceptance from your organization.

In Helen's case, the situation worked out beautifully. She was in a great place in her career at a large pharmaceutical company when she married at age thirty. She continued to excel even after the birth of her first child several years later. She was able to manage her position with the support of her husband and the help of a nanny. After her second child was born, things got tougher to balance. She thought about her options, and decided she'd like to try working three days a week. After talking with her boss and determining that he and company policy would support and encourage her decision, she cut back to what her company terms "100 percent of the effort, 60 percent of the time." She's constantly busy and it's a struggle to stay organized, but she is happy with the balance she's struck. She gets to spend extra time with her small children while she continues on her career path. She'll see how things go in order to decide when to return to work on a full-time basis.

Unfortunately, many companies don't have policies in place to accommodate the needs of working mothers. A finance executive told us, "I had really long hours at work. I also had two kids and a lot of travel. I was told I could work at home—but it couldn't be official because they didn't want to set a precedent. Imagine, my clients and staff couldn't be told I was working two days a week at home—it was crazy." She got what she needed, but it was unofficial, caused unnecessary confusion, and left her feeling like she was doing something wrong.

How to Stay in the Game

Even in companies where flexible working arrangements are available, our research uncovered problems. Women were reluctant to participate, feeling that management, as well as other employees, would perceive them as being less committed to their careers and the company. In addition, women frequently felt that they were doing the equivalent of full-time work for part-time pay. They were concerned that by participating in programs with flexible hours, they would marginalize their positions.

If you're concerned about negatively affecting your career, there are steps you can take to combat this problem:

Produce high-quality work. No matter how many hours you put in, whether from home or the office, continuing to produce an excellent work product and results will go a long way in maintaining your impact.

Volunteer for high-profile assignments. Part-time or full-time, the key projects will keep you noticed by the people who matter. Stay on top of what is going on in your company so you can volunteer when projects come along.

Be there, and be flexible. Even if Thursday is your day off, find a way to adjust your schedule if an important meeting is scheduled on that day. Your presence is a reminder of your role within the company and your flexibility will make your special arrangement less obvious.

Think positive. If you think of your working arrangement as a step backward or a failure, it will come through to others. Stay upbeat. Encourage other women who are struggling with the dilemma of balancing children and working. Share strategies that have worked for you.

Mum's the word. Don't advertise your flexible arrangement to people who don't need to know. It doesn't add anything positive, and you never know who might consider it a negative. Instead of drawing attention to the *way* you work, talk about the things you are doing at work.

Match your pay to your effort. If you feel you're putting in more hours than you're being paid for, evaluate whether it's due to your compulsive work habits or the company's demands. If so, straighten it out to be equitable *and* to maintain your self-worth.

Time off can also be time well spent. If you don't feel positive about your job, you are more likely to make the decision to take a break. After all the pros and cons, it comes down to the question: do I want to continue the struggle to balance my present job with the rest of my life? If the answer is no, you can put the time off to good use. There are a number of career opportunities inherent in taking time off. If you are not truly happy in your current position, this could be the ideal time to make the change you've only thought about.

You might redirect your skills by returning to school or researching new career opportunities. This worked well for Madeline, who was not particularly happy with her work and the direction her career was going. After she had her second child, she decided to take the opportunity to leave her position and return to graduate school. Though money was tight, it made sense because she was able to spend time with her children during most of the day and study when they napped. She scheduled classes in the evenings when her husband was home. Her time off from working allowed her to get the degree necessary to redirect her career. After three years, she received her master's degree and began job hunting. She found a great position that utilized her graduate education, and returned to work full-time when her children started school.

If you decide to leave the job market for a period of time, it's important to have a strategy for returning to work. Without taking the steps to stay current with your industry or profession, gain additional experience, and enhance your skills while you're out, you may not be able to get back in when and where you want.

You can keep your skills alive through work with nonprofit organizations, schools, or other types of volunteer work—and make contacts in the process. Beth was on maternity leave from her job as corporate development manager at a pharmaceutical company when she was introduced to the executive director of a local nonprofit organization. The longtime board member knew that Beth had experience in grant writing, which was vital to getting the funds necessary to provide services to the community. The organization welcomed her skills as a volunteer and quickly discovered how talented she was. The experience was extremely gratifying to Beth—she was able to do most of the writing at home, and the organization highly valued her skills. She soon became a key member of the organization and planned on continuing her involvement, as a board member, when she returned to work.

Even when you're working part-time, or taking time off from work, you're no doubt busy 24/7, and it's hard to make time for community volunteer activities. We all seem to be multitasking at every stage of our lives! If you get into one or two community activities early in your career, it will be easier to incorporate them, both philosophically and practically, into your work and personal life. Typically, there is a little more time earlier in your career for an outside activity, and it is also a time when you are developing habits and patterns of behavior that may stay with you. If you wait until you're in a senior position, with multiple job and home commitments, you may find you need to be more creative in squeezing in new activities.

Every woman's story and situation is different. The more you gain insight and information from talking to others, reading and observing, the more equipped you'll be to make good decisions. Get all the information you can in order to gain a balanced perspective—and more balance in your life.

7

Present Yourself with Impact and Presence
Influence Others with an Enhanced Appearance and Manner

AS SHE PREPARED for her presentation, Marie realized that she was about to lead the most important meeting of her career. As executive vice president of a large bank, she had been a key member of the team who had made the difficult decision to cut nine hundred people from the workforce. She now had the unpleasant responsibility of communicating the why and how of the situation to eighty senior managers whose job it would be to inform those affected. She thought about what her audience was thinking and feeling: What key questions and concerns did they have? And what did they want and need to hear from her? She'd been with the bank for more than fifteen years, and felt that she understood her people's complex mix of emotions, which included anger, frustration, and sadness.

As she walked into the room, Marie touched the shoulders of some of the managers and leaned over to say a few words to others. She retained her poise and strength as she noted the many familiar faces in the audience, which appeared uncertain and anxious. Dressed in a dark suit, her look was somber but powerful. She knew everyone needed to see her composure. She reached the podium, instinctively walked in front of it and asked, "Can you all hear me without a microphone?" After seeing the nods, even in the back, she began to speak directly to the group, without using notes, in a commanding yet sensitive manner. In a strong voice, she gave them the reasons for the decision to downsize and what it meant in practical terms. She acknowledged their concerns, and said she shared many of their feelings, but expressed her confidence in a bright future for the bank.

Every person in the room was listening intently as Marie finished her presentation. She had shown true leadership under difficult circumstances and nearly everyone left feeling better and more confident than when they'd come in. Appearance, manner, and speech are key elements in influencing the way you are perceived by others. In Marie's case, these qualities all worked together to achieve her goal of being a leader in a time of crisis. She had considered her audience, understood their concerns, and thought about what they needed to hear and how to connect with them.

Let's dig deeper. What really worked for Marie? And why, a year later, do people still remember her words that day?

- She mirrored the emotions in the room through her body language, demeanor, and eye contact.
- She used her voice effectively by lowering her pitch and modulating her delivery.
- She dressed formally in a navy skirt suit appropriate for the occasion.
- She set an intimate, personal tone with everyone in the room by her shoulder and arm touches on the way in.
- She timed her entrance impeccably, waiting until everyone was seated.

These are some of the elusive qualities that give a woman the impact and presence to have a significant and positive influence on others.

Having strong leadership qualities like Marie's will serve you well in good times as well as difficult ones. Let's review the most important ones while reflecting on whether you consciously or unconsciously employ some or all of them.

Top Ten Leadership Qualities

1. *Tune in to Others.* Before you hold a meeting or address a group, consider everyone's point of view and what they may be thinking about the

agenda or subject matter. Be sensitive to issues or events that may influence their feelings. Instead of simply steamrolling through your agenda, show that you are collaborative by directly addressing their issues and concerns, asking clarifying questions, and actively listening to their thoughts.

2. *Be Trustworthy.* Engender trust by doing what you say you're going to do, removing yourself from the petty squabbles, staying above the fray, and being genuine. Without trust, those around you will not have confidence in you as a leader. Factors which lead to a lack of trust for a leader include gossiping, backstabbing, revealing confidences, and bad-mouthing people. If you want to be a leader, act like one.

3. *Stay Open-Minded.* Keep your personal biases in check so that you are open to hearing others when they voice their thoughts and opinions. A leader is someone who is willing to hear everyone out and, only after considering the viewpoints of others, to make a fair decision. To do this, stay open-minded and flexible, and use your listening skills when others speak.

4. *Be Decisive.* After a reasonable amount of debate on a subject, it's time to weigh in with your decision. If, after hearing the views of others, you are still uncertain about what to do, you run the risk of being seen as ineffective. Or, if you keep waffling, based on the persuasive powers of the last person in your office, you'll be viewed as indecisive. A leader has the difficult task of listening, assimilating the information, and then making her best judgment.

5. *Communicate.* True leaders are effective communicators in good times as well as bad. Even if you don't have all the answers, or there's bad news to report, it is imperative to maintain consistent communication with employees. People need to hear from their leaders, especially in times of crisis. If you don't have an answer, commit to finding out and getting back to the person when you do.

6. *Roll up Your Sleeves.* While delegation is an important and necessary skill, in challenging times a leader sometimes needs to get down in the trenches with her team. Rolling up your sleeves and being seen as a hands-on manager in a crisis or high-pressure situation will go a long way in motivating your staff. You will command their respect and not be seen as a prima donna.

7. *Grace under Pressure.* Even in the face of adversity, your job as a leader is to calm and inspire those around you. While you may be as upset as anyone about the loss of a large client, a change in senior management,

or your company's acquisition, you're paid to maintain your composure, communicate the message consistent with senior management's, and show maturity to your staff as well as those above you.

8. *Take Risks.* Are you bold enough to go out on a limb? Are you willing to step up and speak out? Risk-taking requires courage—whether you take on an assignment that stretches your skills, put yourself on the line with a daring idea, or disagree with the group if you see things going in the wrong direction. In order to grow and gain respect, it is important to be willing to take calculated risks and brave enough to face rejection.

9. *Have a Vision.* Develop a vision for your area of responsibility. Where do you see your division going? Expand your thinking beyond the tactical and have a clear idea of the "big picture." Think about where you're leading your group, why you're headed in that direction, and what the company's overall strategy is. It's up to you to help others see your "vision" so they understand their contribution to the larger goal. Repeat your vision at the beginning and end of meetings, so your staff is always reminded of where you—and they—are going.

10. *Tap into Strengths.* Are you aware of people's major strengths? Can you identify them in your team members? Once you pinpoint these areas, it will enable you to more effectively tap into your available resources. By being perceptive about those around you and what they bring to the table, you'll be able to develop your people by building on their strengths and putting together more effective working teams.

Tip: Leadership Is Never Saying You're Sorry

Men don't apologize—and neither should women in a corporate setting. Saying "I'm sorry" is viewed as weakness, not politeness. If you've made a mistake, just say, "My data was faulty—here are the correct numbers." Or, if you've arrived late for a meeting, grab a seat and join the discussion. Don't make excuses. Remember, leadership is an ongoing process. The good news is that one mistake isn't fatal to your career.

Women and Leadership

To develop confidence in your leadership ability, take the time to think about the things you do well, how hard you've worked to get where you are, and all the abilities you have. So many times women are more eager to list their deficiencies rather than their strengths, which makes them sound neurotic and erodes others' confidence in their abilities. You must believe in yourself, recognize the value of your skills and talents, and instead of dwelling on what you perceive as faults, recognize and accentuate the positive. Each of us has special gifts and once you find and acknowledge yours, you'll be able to draw strength from them. And, if you're asked to do something you are not good at, overcome your fears. Be clever and find the resources you need to help you, and do it well, no matter what issues you may have encountered in the past.

Tip: Be Confident, Not Cocky

Don't confuse confidence with overconfidence, which can be seen as cockiness. Confidence comes from being comfortable with yourself—who you are, what you've accomplished, and where you're headed. Speak with authority, not arrogance. Show that you're at ease with important people, without excluding others. If you project a know-it-all attitude, or are dismissive of others' ideas and opinions, you will be seen as overconfident, aloof, and ultimately, as having self-esteem issues.

It's often difficult for women to establish their authority. They've frequently told me, in coaching situations, "I think I know what leadership looks like, but I'm not sure I'm personally able to do it." This is because it's more difficult for many to envision a woman in a leadership role. Many of our leaders are "gray-at-the-temples" males, and we have fewer opportunities to see women leaders in action. Look around and observe the style and behavior of successful women leaders to learn what works, and what doesn't. Study how others present themselves, how they connect with others, and how their appearance reflects their confidence. Then start determining what fits with your own personal leadership style.

To do this, choose three women who have qualities that you (and others) admire. Don't limit yourself to people you know personally—include politicians, television personalities, business leaders, and corporate executives you have the opportunity to observe up close or from afar. Make notes on the qualities you'd like to learn from and perhaps emulate. Here are two examples.

Women with Impact and Presence: Examples

Example 1. Gloria Borger, news analyst on CNN

Appearance:	She has a youthful, stylish look, not too much jewelry, sleek hair, wears tasteful outfits with accents of color.
Communication:	She's very direct and knowledgeable about her subjects. She speaks with authority and doesn't appear to use notes.
Connecting with others:	She engages with others, making eye contact and looking directly at them.
Key "charismatic" attribute:	She appears to be interested in, and passionate about, her subjects. She comes across as pleasant, with a sense of humor and great smile.

Example 2. Lynn Pierce, CEO of Riley Consulting Group

Appearance:	She exudes confidence and is extremely well-groomed, everything in place, wears "important" skirt suits, usually with a pin on her lapel.
Communication:	She's gentle yet firm in her style. She speaks up in meetings and people look forward to her comments.
Connecting with others:	She looks you in the eye and, using a bit of southern charm, makes people feel welcome and important. When she enters a room, she confidently and naturally gravitates to the important people there.
Key "charismatic" attribute:	She is strong and authoritative, yet very open and accessible. People believe she has the ability to make things happen. She is not afraid to question the status quo or initiate change.

We've listed examples based on the women *we* analyzed. Now it's your turn to choose three women you most admire for their impact and presence.

Women with Impact and Presence

Name:

Appearance:

Communication:

Connecting with others:

Key "charismatic" attribute:

Name:

Appearance:

Communication:

Connecting with others:

Key "charismatic" attribute:

Name:

Appearance:

Communication:

Connecting with others:

Key "charismatic" attribute:

What have you learned from this exercise? Complete the exercise below to help you define the traits and characteristics that you admire in the women you've listed and those that you should focus on for yourself.

Building Greater Impact and Presence

List the main traits shared by your three women, for example:

> Confidence
> Connects with people
> Well groomed
> Well dressed
> Authoritative
> Feminine
> Good communicator

What characteristics have you seen in each that most appeal to you? For example:

> Confidence
> Connects with people
> Authoritative, yet feminine
> Good communicator

Of the characteristics that appeal to you, which ones do you possess? For example:

> Connects with people
> Feminine
> Good communicator

Which characteristics do you aspire to have? For example:

> Confidence
> Being Authoritative

Now make your list based on the women *you* selected.

List the main traits shared by your three women:

What characteristics have you seen in each that most appeal to you?

Of the characteristics that appeal to you, which ones do you possess?

Which characteristics do you aspire to?

Mix and match to create impact and presence . . .

Barbara, an accountant at a Big 4 firm, was an astute observer of style and often tried out different techniques she had seen other leaders use which impressed her. For instance, she learned from her last boss to effectively use long pauses in meetings with clients, to see if they had anything more to say before jumping in. She also developed a sense of humor that made people feel more comfortable with her, modeling this after a mentor she had watched who was well liked by colleagues. Finally, she perfected her eye contact so people felt she was really connecting with them, a skill she adopted from a consultant she knew who was a great people person. There is nothing wrong with modeling your style and behavior after more than one person, as Barbara did. As you fine-tune your own leadership style, it's okay to try out what works for others and see if it fits your style. If you feel comfortable with it, incorporate it—if it doesn't feel right, discard it.

Impact and Presence Checklist

Let's continue our exploration of what leadership impact and presence look like for you. When we asked corporate executives to describe the traits of a woman in their company whom they consider a leader, the following words were used over and over in their descriptions. Give yourself a report card on how you think you stack up.

On a scale of 1 to 3, where 1 = never, 2 = sometimes, and 3 = always, rate yourself on whether these characteristics apply to you.

Able	___	Energetic	___	Polished	___
Calm	___	Enthusiastic	___	Positive	___
Charismatic	___	Flexible	___	Risk Taking	___
Collaborative	___	Genuine	___	Strong	___
Collegial	___	Honest	___	Tactful	___
Confident	___	Inspiring	___	Team Player	___
Consistent	___	Intelligent	___	Trusted	___
Creative	___	Mature	___	Wise	___
Egalitarian	___	Motivational	___		
Empathetic	___	Open	___		

You should have scored a 3 in a number of areas. If you have not scored a 3 in some areas that you consider important to your career, you may want to get more feedback or do some individual work on these. If you scored a 2 and want to improve to a 3 in specific categories, work selectively in these areas. If you have rated yourself as a 1 in a number of areas, you have a great deal of work to do to improve your leadership abilities. Choose what you consider the most important and get started.

Find Out How You're Perceived

If you are having difficulty with your self-appraisal, or think you're on target but want to confirm your own opinion, get more objective, third-party feedback. Without a realistic reading on your own impact and knowing how you come across, it's hard to make positive steps to change. There are several ways to get the feedback on how you're perceived as a leader.

Option One

Ask your human resources department to perform a 360-degree review, which is a series of interviews conducted by a human resources professional or third party with people whom you work for and with, and those who work for you. Questions are posed about your work style and the results are compiled into a confidential report. You can approach the HR department and say, for example:

> I'm working on my career development and leadership skills, and think it would be very helpful to get feedback from others I work with. I know that one way to do this is to conduct a 360-degree review. Is this something the company could do for me?

If your company cannot perform this service or get someone from the outside to do it, ask them for their advice on how else you could get the type of feedback you're looking for. It may involve improvising a little and collecting data yourself from your colleagues. You could, for example, talk to them about the outcome of a recent project you were involved in and get feedback on ways the process could have been improved.

Jan, who runs a research group for a major consumer goods company, heard a lot of good news from her 360-degree review, and she also received some feedback that caused her to think and take action. Her strengths were many—she was seen by others as the successor to her boss, and an enthusiastic team player who was liked and highly respected for her technical expertise.

Her peers and colleagues, however, commented that she often appeared disorganized, seemingly because she took on too many assignments. She also received feedback that she was seen as fun-loving and playful—which they appreciated in social situations—but that she was not serious enough in more formal settings. In her presentations, she didn't connect with her audiences because her voice was nasal and flat, and she tended to look at the presentation on the screen instead of the people in the room. All of these areas, when improved, would lead to her becoming a stronger leader.

Jan resisted the urge to be offended—she knew the feedback she received was constructive and honest. When she thought about it, these were all things she knew she could work on and change. Armed with this determination, she took a number of steps to develop her leadership qualities.

- She analyzed her communication style by being videotaped, and practiced improvements to her presentation style.

- She developed a greater awareness of being a leader and tempered her sense of humor, developed a tighter agenda in meetings, and expanded her knowledge of other areas of the company.
- She worked with her boss on the issues of taking on too much and delegated more to her staff. They even developed a signal he could use in meetings to warn her against over-volunteering for initiatives and projects.
- With the help of her administrative assistants, she reviewed her work to delegate what she could, attend only necessary meetings, and streamline her paperwork.

Jan's executive style has really improved, and she has now carved out the time—and developed the expertise—to do more speaking engagements, creating visibility for her company and herself.

Option Two

Ask if your company can arrange for you to work with a coach. Most companies use external coaches for leadership development because they have the skills, training, objectivity, and time to work with the employee. In this case, you can raise the subject with human resources and say:

> I have thought a lot about where I'm going in my career, and there are several things that I'd like to work on in the area of leadership development. I thought it might be helpful to have a coach—could you help me identify someone I could work with?

When Monica met with her boss, instead of a glowing review, he told her that in the past several months her work had been slipping and she was not seen as effective in her leadership. Monica had advanced very rapidly to her current level, getting several promotions in only three years. Her boss was frank in telling her that she appeared to be out of her league in areas like managing people and organization skills, and she projected an arrogance that put people off. He suggested that a coach might be helpful in getting Monica back in the right direction and that she should contact human resources.

After talking with Monica, the human resources manager realized that she needed to match Monica carefully with a coach for the experience to be successful. She selected a qualified coach who also had appropriate work experience and familiarity with their industry, and arranged for Monica to meet her. The first meeting dealt with Monica's discomfort with coaching— she'd never done it and was openly skeptical. Her coach was able to calm her fears and gain her trust, and as Monica's receptivity increased, they were able to work on Monica's issues related to leadership style, attitude, and thoroughness. Because it was a good match, Monica and her coach developed a positive relationship. Through their work together, she became more well-liked by colleagues, organized, and effective in her leadership style and communication.

Option Three

If you don't succeed in your actions with the human resources department, or your company is too small to support these initiatives, your next option is to ask your boss or mentor for feedback. You could ask him or her in this way:

> I'm trying to continue my leadership development and I feel that it would be helpful to get feedback. If I outline some areas where I think I need to fine-tune my style and build my effectiveness, could you tell me how you and others view my performance in these areas, and give me your thoughts on how to improve?

In some cases, bosses can be excellent advisors and mentors. Sara's boss was a natural "coach" and took serious interest in her career from the day he hired her. Even when Sara was no longer reporting to him, her former boss gave her feedback and advice whenever she needed it. He continued to help her in evaluating situations, defining the leadership qualities that were required, and seeing how others were viewing things. For instance, when she was uncertain about how the CEO felt about a project she was working on, he was able to steer her in the right direction. She felt like she could always approach him for his thoughts and come away with additional knowledge and insight.

Option Four

Find an image consultant who can give you professional and objective advice about your image, appearance, and style. Unlike a coach, an image consultant gives more limited feedback, which centers only on the external "package" you present. This can be very helpful in improving your presence. If you don't know of an image consultant, there are several ways to find one. You can check the membership directory of the local Chamber of Commerce or professional women's group, or ask friends if they know anyone. Another option is to inquire at a couple of high-end department stores that offer personal shoppers. Ask for information on the services they offer (they might have someone on staff who is qualified to help you) or if they could connect you with someone for the services you need. Ideally, the qualifications you are looking for in an image consultant include having experience with women in the business world, and having the ability to make suggestions on clothing, hair, makeup and general style compatible with your position, appearance, and checkbook.

Julie had been a regional manager for a small local credit union, and when it was acquired by a larger institution, she was given significant additional responsibilities and a promotion in title. After attending several introductory meetings with the larger financial institution's personnel, she felt that she needed a more polished look to fit with the style of her new organization. She began working with an image consultant recommended by a friend, and had dramatic results. She got new glasses that were much more stylish and becoming, lightened her hair, added more color and sophistication to her wardrobe, and arranged to work out weekly. Her physical workouts made her look better and feel more energetic. She says that modifying her look and style changed the way people viewed her and contributed to her career success. She has since moved into an even bigger role, and feels as powerful and terrific as she looks.

Tip: Dress Down—But Not Too Far Down

Take advantage of a dress-down code if the company has one, but be careful not to carry the informality too far. Women who aspire to more senior roles should dress a notch higher than their peers. This sets an example for employees and makes an impression on higher-ups. Wear casual pants, not jeans, and keep a neutral suit jacket in your office to dress up your outfit. Even on dress-down days, be sure your dress is professional enough to attend an impromptu meeting with an important client or the boss.

Whichever option you choose, after you have received feedback on how you're perceived as a leader, return to the three women you listed earlier as having impact and presence. Review the characteristics that you said you possess and aspire to in your self-analysis, and compare them with how other people have described you in the feedback you received.

Where are the commonalities? Did the feedback of others match your self-analysis? Where are the gaps? Pick the two or three leadership characteristics that you believe are realistic for you to work on, and develop a plan for each.

My Leadership Characteristics (Example)

Characteristics I Aspire to: **Feedback I Received:**
1. Good communication style   Need better presentation skills

Since there was a gap in what she thought, and how she was perceived, she's created the plan below to improve her communication:

My Leadership Plan (Example)

Characteristic to be improved: Communication and presentation style
My plan to improve: I will videotape myself giving a presentation to determine my problem areas. I will then critique myself with the help of a friend and decide whether to engage a speech consultant to improve my presentation skills.

Now make your own list, and plans. This analysis should give you a road map for what you need to work on and improve in order to have more impact and presence.

Ten Ways for Women to Project Impact and Presence

In addition to the top leadership qualities we've reviewed, there are a number of intangible qualities that will add to your impact and presence by creating "charisma." These won't be found in most standard leadership training programs, but it would be wise to emphasize these qualities if you already have one or two, or develop those that are compatible with your personality and style.

1. *Get Personal.* Take the time to send a note to your employees or colleagues on a job well done. Make a note of the names of the children of your employees, boss, and colleagues and refer to them by name. Send a card or flowers on a significant occasion. In short, display a personal

My Leadership Characteristics

Characteristics to which I aspire: Feedback I have received:

1. _____   _____

2. _____   _____

3. _____   _____

4. _____   _____

5. _____   _____

My Leadership Plan

1st characteristic to be improved:
My plan to improve:

2nd characteristic to be improved:
My plan to improve:

3rd characteristic to be improved:
My plan to improve:

and thoughtful touch in your relationships. It will pay off in building morale, cementing relationships, and encouraging high performance from your employees.

2. *Demonstrate an Interest.* Ask an employee "How are you doing?" and wait for an answer. Look people in the eye and acknowledge them when you pass. Ask where you can be of help to others. If colleagues or staff are working on a project you've been involved with, ask how it's going. Connect with people and show a genuine interest.

3. *Show Your Enthusiasm.* Be upbeat in your demeanor—have a positive cadence to your voice and a great smile. Don't bring your bad mood or

family problems to work. Enthusiasm is contagious—people naturally want to be part of the world of someone who sees things positively and optimistically.

4. *Keep up Appearances.* By looking good every day, you set an example and show those around you that you care about your appearance. It also helps you feel good about yourself. Scrutinize everything from your hair to your nails to your clothes. Whether it's a dress-up or dress-down day, make sure your appearance demonstrates your pride in yourself.

5. *Make Things Happen.* Be the type of person who is known for "doing" by jumping into a project or initiative. Show that you're an action person, not just someone who talks a good game and gets everyone else to do the work. If you're in a lull at work, find a project to jump into to keep your energy going.

6. *Be a Thought Leader.* Stay current with trends and events in your industry, read newspapers and magazines, and you'll be more engaging as a conversationalist. Participate in seminars and conferences where you can be exposed to new ideas for your business. Being well rounded will lead you to generate interesting ideas that capture the imagination of others. Bring your good ideas to the office for discussion.

7. *Develop a Powerful Aura.* Develop your own powerful blend of femininity, professionalism, and authority in your clothing, style, and communication. Consider your personality, position, and corporate culture. Look at your corporate environment and the styles of other leaders to determine what kind of executive style will work for you.

8. *Know Who You Are.* Having your priorities straight and your life in perspective will keep you centered and able to handle whatever arises. If you're not in control, people will feel your stress. Having self-confidence about who you are will project to others and lead them to have confidence in you. Drawing from your inner knowledge will help you guide others.

9. *Start the Day Right.* Make the effort to greet people as you come in every morning. Smile, and acknowledge them without being overbearing, since not everyone is a "morning person." Be personable and pleasant— it sets the right tone for starting the day's work, no matter what problems may lie ahead. A leader is instrumental in setting the tone and mood.

10. *Walk the Halls.* Take a break and step out of your office several times a day for a stroll down the hall. Seeing and chatting briefly with the manager or boss is motivating for people. Pop in here and there, and others will feel included and motivated. You may also pick up some good

information on your walks. It's positive to get out and see—and be seen—by others.

Tip: Leave Your Troubles at the Door

Whether your twins are in hot water over a school prank, your husband's job is shaky, or your close friend has just learned she has a serious illness, there's no room for moodiness in the office. Handle these problems on your own time even if it feels like your life is fraying at the seams. Let your coworkers try to figure out how you keep everything in your life running smoothly. If you need to take a day off to take care of yourself—do it.

The Road to Success

Now that you've done the exercises in this chapter and understand your leadership qualities and presence, take the following quizzes. Let's see if you've really put it all together and reached true leadership.

What does your leadership style say about you?	Yes	No
1. Do you consider the concerns and motivations of others before speaking?	☐	☐
2. Are you seen as a person to be trusted with confidences and information?	☐	☐
3. Do you think about how you will display your leadership qualities before entering a room?	☐	☐
4. Do you evaluate situations and people fairly?	☐	☐
5. Are you seen as a collaborative team player?	☐	☐
6. Are you willing to roll up your sleeves and chip in on whatever needs to be done?	☐	☐
7. Do others voice respect and admiration for you?	☐	☐
8. Do you maintain a calm, strong exterior, especially in difficult situations?	☐	☐
9. Are you able to be flexible when facts and circumstances change?	☐	☐
10. Are you willing to take calculated risks?	☐	☐
11. Are you known to be a person of integrity?	☐	☐
12. Do you have a vision for your team and yourself which you communicate and follow consistently?	☐	☐

How many yeses did you get? If it's more than five, you have positive leadership traits and need to focus on them to continue growing your leadership profile. If you have fewer than five yeses, you need to work on how you relate and project yourself to others.

Have you reached a position of true leadership?	*Yes*	*No*
1. Is your opinion sought before decisions are made?	☐	☐
2. Are you quoted by others in your company?	☐	☐
3. Are you included in strategic meetings?	☐	☐
4. Is your involvement sought on projects, initiatives, and causes?	☐	☐
5. Are you included in informal discussions?	☐	☐
6. Do people ask you to mentor them?	☐	☐
7. Is your style emulated by others in your organization?	☐	☐

If you answered yes to four or more, you're in a leadership role whether you know it or not—congratulations! If not, use your powers of observation and self-evaluation techniques to see what other leaders do to establish credibility that you don't. Evaluate your key relationships and connect with your company's senior leaders. Get involved in strategic projects and demonstrate your capabilities.

Tip: Build on Your Strengths

If you're a fountain of knowledge in your subject area, but feel uncomfortable with your appearance, draw on your technical expertise to project strength and determination on the outside. Square your shoulders, hold your head high, and dress like an executive. Or, if you feel great about your "power look" but are a bundle of nerves inside, take three deep cleansing breaths, look in the mirror and tell yourself that people can't see your nervousness, only your great exterior.

You may find that the road to success has a way of sneaking up on you—and that the qualities you've been trying so hard to develop, the community activities to which you've devoted yourself, and all the networking you've done have paid off. All of a sudden, you realize you have been given significant responsibility and are held in high regard. You've achieved what you set out to do! When you reach this pivotal juncture, it's more important than ever to continue to follow through and set an example by analyzing, maintaining, and refining your leadership qualities.

One way to enhance your leadership role is to become a leader in the community as well as in the executive suite. To do this, women must be seen as powerful forces—and power and money go hand in hand. Have you ever noticed that most of the prestigious business awards are given to men who head companies, chair boards of directors, and give—literally—to the community? Men hold 90 percent of CEO positions and have great resources at their disposal, which they are able to use to effectively command influence. They are able to have their companies underwrite events, sponsor causes, and contribute resources throughout the community.

Though there is great potential for women to take their places as influential donors since we control the majority of wealth in the United States, it has not happened as of yet. This greatly affects the way women are seen in the business world.

Though you may not be in the "big leagues," it's important to use the resources you have available to make a difference and increase your impact. These resources include your time, talent, and any personal funds you can and want to give. A recent fund-raising effort for the United Way brought women together with the goal of increasing women's awareness of the importance of philanthropy. A major event was held and attendees were asked to give at least $1,000. The response was enthusiastic and the results were impressive. A large number of women contributors became more actively involved in the organization, raising millions of dollars for the many causes it supports. This gave them more clout on the strategic direction of the organization and over time, these women will have greater influence in such areas as board selection and effecting social change.

In addition to using your personal resources, you'll want to utilize your company's name, influence, and capital to maximum advantage when possible. Most mid- to large-size companies have funds set aside for charitable giving and underwriting of events. Find out what's available to you and how you can tap into these funds—then be strategic about how to use them. This will enhance your and your company's community standing.

Amanda, who is president of a division of a large insurance company, holds an important position which gives her generous resources to utilize in the community. She has an annual budget of $500,000 which is to be used to enrich the community and raise the profile of her institution. This gives her power and influence, since she is able to decide where and when to spend her budget. She is asked to contribute to many causes and sit on a number of boards, but she is highly strategic and thoughtful about where she puts her time and money, in accordance with the mission of her company. These are key business decisions that can make or break her company, as well as her reputation and future career. Luckily for her community, Amanda is smart and hard working and in addition to her financial resources, she gives her time generously.

To get to the position of true leadership, women must start to become more active in organizations, make strategic contacts, and work their way up, and then out—to new and different *nonprofit* and *for-profit* organizations. In order to achieve the power and status of becoming directors of for-profit and large nonprofit boards, women have to start by joining smaller and less prestigious nonprofit organizations and working their way up.

As of now, women don't have a real voice in how companies and organizations are run. Because there are not enough women in positions of power on boards of directors, they aren't involved in setting strategy, managing finances, and selecting leadership. *Not only would a shift in the numbers help women in their careers, but it would be valuable to the boards they serve.* Most women instinctively take responsibilities seriously, and become active board members with the integrity and courage to ask the tough questions—remember who blew the whistle on the high-profile company scandals? Women did!

As more and more companies recognize the power of women as consumers of their products and services, they will be compelled to include more women on their boards. So, decide what your interests and goals are and position yourself to be selected when the timing is right by getting the experience you need now. That experience, combined with a commanding presence and leadership style, will make you a person who is respected and sought after.

C H A P T E R **8**

Keep Your Career on Track
Set Goals and Manage Your Success

YOU CAN DO all the things we recommend, work your tail off, and still have a job that isn't working for you. Maybe it's your boss, the culture, or the job match. Though there may be many reasons to stay where you are, if your job is unfulfilling or keeping you from your career goals, don't make excuses—make a move. Take a look at what's going on, explore various options, and plan accordingly. Remember, *you* are in control of your career.

Bonnie was highly motivated and had been working on her leadership development skills with extra zeal since she'd received a company promotion a year ago to director of research. After getting feedback from her boss that she was not always clearly understood, she had fine-tuned her communication skills and style by getting herself videotaped and making necessary improvements. Though Bonnie was active in community activities, had established good contacts internally and externally, and made sure that key people in her company knew of her accomplishments, she noticed one of her colleagues had been promoted about six months ago and was now in charge of an important and interesting company initiative she wasn't involved in. Her last review with her boss was lukewarm, the raise that accompanied it was small, and though she wasn't sure why, she seemed stalled in her career.

As she analyzed the situation, she thought about what had changed over the past several months in her position and her company, and a couple of ideas came to mind. The promotion had put her in a more significant managerial role, so she was no longer running the research projects that had led to her promotion. Instead, she was managing the people running the projects. She remembered, too, that at her last review her boss had reminded her that the other research directors had advanced technological and scientific degrees, so her education, which was limited to an undergraduate degree, was not comparable to her peers.

Bonnie added it up and understood why her career was stalled. She'd gotten off track with her promotion to manager, and was academically underqualified for her position. She'd loved it when she had a more hands-on role with the research projects, and her promotion had removed her from that function. In addition, she hadn't taken steps to get the graduate degree that was needed for her to advance in her company, which had become larger and more sophisticated in its talent needs. Bonnie had moved ahead in her career—right into a stone wall.

Many people get promoted and find themselves no longer doing the work they most enjoy doing and do best. We allow our company or circumstance to decide where we should be placed and how we should be utilized. Then, as in Bonnie's case, all of a sudden you realize that you're on a different career track than you intended or studied for. If this is the case for you, the first step is to analyze your current situation to try and pinpoint whether your career has stalled or derailed, and why. Take the quiz to determine if you're on or off track.

Is your job or career off track?	Yes	No
1. Are you frequently unhappy when you go to work?	☐	☐
2. Has your career taken an unexpected downturn or detour?	☐	☐
3. Do you ever miss the work you did in your earlier positions?	☐	☐
4. Were you happier then?	☐	☐
5. Do you often feel frustration with your work?	☐	☐
6. Do you feel you are stagnating in your position?	☐	☐
7. Do you lack interest in many of your projects?	☐	☐
8. Do you feel ill-equipped to deal with your job responsibilities?	☐	☐
9. Has it been over six months since you've received positive feedback on your performance?	☐	☐
10. Are other colleagues advancing in their careers while you are stalled?	☐	☐

If you've answered yes to three or more of the questions, your career may be off track. You have some real work to do in managing and planning your future to get back on track. For example, if your career took a downturn or detour, think about what happened and when. If you used to be happier in your work, think about why. If you have fewer than three yeses, it sounds like your career may be on track for now—read on for information on how to keep it that way.

Are you in trouble? If you've found yourself questioning your career path, take a hard look at what's been occurring at your company and with your position, and try to put it in perspective. Here are some areas to consider.

1. *Advancement.* Think about your last promotion and salary increase. How long has it been since you received a promotion? When did you last receive a raise—and how did it compare to company guidelines? Have your colleagues been promoted while you have not? Are you as qualified as they are? Do you feel you have the right skills, abilities, and experience to advance? Have you clearly communicated your interest and qualifications for promotion to the key people responsible? If you are unsure of the answers to these questions, discuss them with your boss or human resources manager.

2. *Feedback.* Have you received feedback about your work lately? Who gave it to you—and was it positive or negative? Has it changed over time? If so, perhaps you can attribute it to a particular incident or circumstance. If you took on a high-profile project a couple of months ago and haven't heard any feedback on your work, think about what that might mean. Consider checking out your results with your boss to see if you're on track. Don't let too much time go by with no feedback—you may be going down the wrong path.

3. *Projects.* Are you included in the interesting, high-profile company projects? Review your work assignments and determine whether they're routine or you're on the receiving end of the important company initiatives. Are you invited to strategic meetings to discuss the future goals of your division or company? If you don't like the results of your self-analysis, discuss the situation with your boss or human resources manager to try to determine what the problem is. If you are not viewed as a high-potential leader, find out why.

4. *Respect.* Do others appear to respect your opinion and seek out your advice? Or have you been shy about offering your opinions, and are not seen as a real player? If you haven't actively been a part of important

meetings, try to be more assertive and step up with some good ideas, and see if things change.

Tip: Don't Stick Your Head in the Sand

Changes in the corporate environment are tough to deal with because they present challenges many people would rather not think about. But the price of ignoring change is high. People who don't pay attention to what's going on around them often find themselves out of a job. Be aware of shifts in technology, direction, focus, philosophy, or vision in your field.

If you think you are in trouble, there are steps to be taken to pinpoint the problem and develop a solution. First, you'll need to decide if the trouble relates to your job, your company, or your career track. Here are examples of each.

Katie was a tremendous salesperson with a great reputation. She had years of experience in selling financial services, which she did enthusiastically and successfully. She was ambitious and had networked her way into a vice president of sales position at a new company, heading up a large sales team, when she ran into trouble. While she was great at selling, Katie was a hopeless motivator and leader for a sales force. She was also rigid, competitive, and inflexible. Her group disliked her intensely and started missing sales targets. It was obvious the position wasn't working out for Katie. Though she was a great salesperson, she wasn't able to translate those skills into leadership and management. The job was all wrong for her, and she left the company for an independent sales position elsewhere which played to her strengths as an individual contributor.

In thinking about your own job:

1. Are you realistic about your strengths and weaknesses? Is your job tapping into your strengths?
2. Is your current job utilizing the same skills that have made you successful in the past?
3. Are you qualified to be promoted to the next level of advancement?

If you've answered no to any of the above, you may be in the wrong job. If this is the case, delve a little deeper by taking a look at your top strengths to see how they match up with your job. Take the top five strengths you listed in chapter 3, "Sell Your Strengths," and list them again, this time adding a list of the top five skills *required in your job*. Do they match up? Do your top skills relate directly to those necessary to do your job, or are the skill sets different? If you and your job are a good match, the two lists of skills will be nearly identical.

Example

	Top Five Skills/Duties Required
My Top Five Strengths:	in My Job:
1. Analyzing numbers	Doing the budget

	Top Five Skills/Duties Required
My Top Five Strengths:	in My Job:
1.	
2.	
3.	
4.	
5.	

If you find your top five strengths are not a match to the top five skills required in your job, you may want to consider other career alternatives and develop a plan to change. If there is a skill missing, consider getting some additional training, coaching, or mentoring in that area. If your strengths match the job skills necessary, your job is not the issue.

Tip: Manage Your Career

Managing your career is a high-stakes game—and no one can do it better than you. Stay current in your skills and abilities in order to be marketable. Know where your gaps in knowledge and education lie— and try to fill them if possible. Make sure your work is tapping into areas where you are strong. Have a career plan and keep your antennae up for changes in your company or industry that may affect you.

Are You in the Wrong Company?

When she was recruited to join a multinational corporation, Erin was ecstatic. She was offered an excellent employment package, a position with a lot of promise, and her new company appeared to be doing well. Two months after she joined, the corporate environment had dramatically changed, and with it came a federal investigation into procedures and practices employed by the company. As Erin learned more, and attended various meetings, it became obvious to her that the leadership of the company was focused on the bottom line to the exclusion of ethics. She was being asked to do things that made her uncomfortable, like changing the way the expenses were categorized. Reluctantly, and with great disappointment, Erin acknowledged that she and the company did not line up from an integrity and values point of view, and that she would be compelled to leave.

In thinking about your company:

1. Do you feel comfortable with your corporate environment?
2. Do your values and work ethic line up with your company's?
3. Do you admire the people running the company?
4. Are you comfortable with your colleagues?

If you've answered no to any of the above, your company may be wrong for you. You'll learn more about company compatibility later in this chapter. We'll discuss matching yourself with your employer, as well as how to know if you should be your own boss. If you've answered yes to all of the above questions, your company is not the issue.

Are You on the Wrong Career Track?

Madeline got into her new sales position by convincing her employer that even though she'd always been in marketing, sales and marketing were closely related and she was strong in both. She was hired as sales manager for a consulting firm with a great salary and the goal of significantly increasing sales. After a substantial training period on the company and its services, Madeline was ready to begin. The problem was, she didn't know where to start. Even with her company training, and self-proclaimed sales expertise, she couldn't figure out how to get her sales effort off the ground. When she looked at her prospect list, she froze. The truth was, though Madeline wanted to be a salesperson—and was good enough to sell herself into her job—she was secretly afraid of rejection and didn't want to take the risks involved in the sales process. She was on the wrong career track.

In thinking of your career:

1. Is your career in line with your skills, personality, and interests?
2. Do your capabilities match up with your job requirements?
3. Is your career satisfying to you?

If you've answered no to any of the above, you may need to rethink your career track and develop a plan for change. If you've answered yes to the above questions, your career track is not the issue.

Get Yourself on Track

Look carefully at the things you do on the job that have made you successful and list the top five. These are things you have learned in your work and when you do them you are almost always successful. Are you doing them in your current job?

Things I Do Well That Have Made Me Successful

Example: I have selected, developed, and retained high-performing people.

1.
2.
3.
4.
5.

Are you currently using at least three of the five that have made you successful in the past? If not, you're running the risk that your current job isn't tapping into what you do best. If your job is not drawing on your strengths, you could eventually fail.

Now, what about your "derailers"? Be honest and list the things you do not do well that could derail your career. If you are having trouble with this, look at your past reviews. Still in trouble? Ask your boss.

Derailers That Could Get in My Way

Example: I have a problem with change—I'm resistant to new ways of doing things.

1.

2.

3.

4.

5.

Are you being asked to do things you're not good at in your current role in your company? Are your derailers in conflict with your company's direction or strategy? If so, you may need to make a change. If you are tapping into your weaknesses, your endeavors could fail.

Long-Term Planning

Strangely, most people don't do career planning until they run into a serious career obstacle. Yet, it's imperative to think about and plan your career as far ahead as possible, so you can gain the skills and experience you'll need to reach your long-term goals.

Tip: Have a Strategy for Success

To reach the top rung of the corporate ladder, develop a strategic career plan and stick to it. Map out what you need to do to reach your goals and stay on course. If you need line experience, get it. If you're asked to relocate for a promotion, do it. If you should change positions to get experience for your future, go ahead. Without a strategy, you could stagnate in positions that don't advance your career.

Where do you want to be in three to five years? What will it take to get there? Scrutinize the qualifications and experience needed, and compare them with your own. Try it with this exercise, which we call the "Reality Check."

Picture your ideal future job position. Then, imagine you are applying to the executive search firm charged with filling this position. What position is it?

My Ideal Position: (in three to five years)

List the five essential qualifications that the search firm would require for this position. For example, would it require international experience? Financial skills? Technical experience? Business development?

Five Essential Qualifications for My Ideal Position

1.

2.

3.

4.

5.

In the space provided under the qualifications on the next page, list two or three accomplishments you have achieved in each area. Start your accomplishment with an action verb and quantify the results of the accomplishment if possible. If you listed "financial skills" as an essential qualification, you might put: "Managed a departmental budget of $2 million," "Earned an MBA in finance," or "Saved the company $3 million in costs by streamlining my department" as accomplishments.

What's missing? Where were you struggling to find an accomplishment? If the executive search firm reviewed your information, would you make the cut or would they find too many gaps? If you don't have any accomplishments in one essential area, that's a gap you'll have to fill to realistically have a chance at your ideal future position. If your accomplishments are weak in some areas, you may need extra experience or training to strengthen your résumé. Once you've identified what's missing, or a weak area, you'll need to develop a plan to fill the gaps, including identifying the resources, people, training, and education to help you.

Where are *your* gaps? Make a list of the top five things you still need to learn. Now, check out this list with your boss and perhaps some other individuals in your company. If they agree on what you still need to learn to achieve your ideal position, develop an action plan for yourself that includes the skills you need to learn, how you will go about learning them, and when this will be accomplished. Although this may leave you with some hard work

Five Essential Qualifications for My Ideal Position

1.
My accomplishments in this area:

    1.

    2.

    3.

2.
My accomplishments in this area:

    1.

    2.

    3.

3.
My accomplishments in this area:

    1.

    2.

    3.

4.
My accomplishments in this area:

    1.

    2.

    3.

5.
My accomplishments in this area:

    1.

    2.

    3.

to do to reach your goal, understand the rewards of taking these steps—and the possible consequences if you don't!

What Do I Still Need to Learn?

Example: I need to learn how to manage a budget.

1.

2.

3.

4.

5.

My Action Plan (Example)

Skills to Learn:	How Will I Learn Them?	When?
1. Budgeting skills	Ask my boss if I can participate in the next budgeting process	4th Q 2009

My Action Plan

Skills to Learn:	How Will I Learn Them?	When?
1.		
2.		
3.		
4.		
5.		

Tip: Not Everyone Wants to Be a Leader

Though everyone can learn leadership skills, it may be that your personality, style, or goals are not compatible with managing a department, division, or company. You may find that the stresses of such a role are too great, and that you would prefer to be an individual contributor. There's nothing wrong with honestly looking at yourself in the mirror and admitting you don't have the ambition or disposition for a top job. Take pride in whatever you do best—and use your leadership ability in that way.

Denise felt that there was a lack of potential for promotion in her present company and was informally keeping her eyes open for other opportunities when she received a call from her former mentor. He had taken an executive position more than a year ago with a regional, privately held company that was now looking for someone with Denise's skills. She agreed to interview for the director of operations position, which was a new one for the fast-growing company. When she met with the executive vice president who would be her boss, he seemed "pre-sold" by her qualifications and Denise was caught off guard by how quickly things moved. He called the next day with an offer, which included the precise salary Denise had requested, and she was thrilled. She thanked him and told him she was very interested, but when she asked if he would be putting the offer in a letter, he was flustered and seemed to view her request as a sign of distrust. Denise explained that this was standard corporate procedure to ensure each understood the employment terms. Though he wasn't particularly gracious about it, her new boss complied and she began her job three weeks later.

Looking back at the process, Denise soon realized it was a precursor of things to come—most of them unpleasant. Her boss was difficult to deal with and the environment turned out to be very unprofessional. Most of the executives had never worked in a corporate environment—her boss's childhood friend owned the company—and any decision making boiled down to the mood of the moment. Compounding the situation, there was no existing budget for her area, and she had to fight for every penny. Denise was angry—mostly with herself. She'd made an assumption that because her mentor was there, it was a good place to work. She hadn't asked the hard questions or done any research on the company.

Tip: Be Sure a "Great Opportunity" Is Great for You

Always do your groundwork before you think of joining a former colleague at another company. Talk to enough people to get a broad view. Be certain that the culture fits with your personality and goals. Make sure you feel comfortable with the company strategy and the people you'll be working with. Make this evaluation for yourself—don't rely on someone else's viewpoint.

If you decide to look externally for career opportunities, be sure you're making a change that is positive. Many women who wouldn't consider purchasing a home or even taking a vacation without careful research neglect to study their potential future employer and have no idea what they're walking into when they accept a job. There are many ways to research a potential new employer—asking direct questions, reading about the company, talking with people who have worked there. Remember, the decision to take a new position goes two ways: the company has to want you, and you have to want them. Here are some issues to think about to have the best chance of success when you make a change. Though it requires some effort, this research will really pay off.

Research a Company Match: What Is the Company Culture?

Management

Is it a public or privately held company?
What is the composition of the board of directors, top officers?
Is management aligned around mutual goals and a common vision?
What is the management style?
Is the company known for its integrity?

Diversity

Is diversity a priority for the company?
Does the company employ "best practices" programs for women?
Has the company been commended for its diversity programs?
What diversity programs does the company offer?
How many women are in the senior ranks?

People

Do employees feel valued and respected?
Is the company known for teamwork and collegiality?
What do ex-employees say about the company?
Are people free to voice their views?

Financial

To what extent does the economy affect the company's business?
Is the company an acquisition target?

Is the industry experiencing problems?

What do financial experts say about the future of the industry?

Are there any investigations of the company or industry in process?

Market Position

What is the company's position in the marketplace?

Are its products and services competitive?

Are there competitor companies with new products in development?

Are there trends or regulatory factors that could negatively impact the company's growth?

To get answers to these questions:

- Ask questions in networking meetings and connect with people who either work at the company or are former employees.
- Send for brochures, annual reports—and any other type of written material published by the company.
- Search online for news articles and press releases about the company. Go back a couple of years and look for trends.
- Check with financial analysts on their projections for the company and industry. This can be done through a stockbroker, investment banker, or industry analyst.

Companies That Offer More for Women

Since so few companies have large numbers of women in the executive ranks, it is difficult to estimate your potential for success based solely on that ratio. If there are no women in senior roles, you may not want to be the one to plow new ground. Another more practical way to gauge an opportunity is to find out what the company offers women in terms of leadership development programs.

The Leader's Edge recently conducted a survey to find out what Fortune 1000 companies are offering their women employees in terms of "best practices programs"—those strategies and tactics employed by the companies to help develop, attract, and retain successful women. These "best practices" include coaching, retention strategies, mentoring, and networking exclusively for women in the company.

When you are contemplating a move to a new company, you'll want to investigate where your potential target companies stand. Do they offer programs—and if so, what are they and who runs them? If you would be one of the only women at your level, you may find that the company is oblivious to key issues that affect women. You can also find out, from reading articles and the annual report, how committed the CEO is to these programs. Our research showed that CEO involvement in diversity efforts such as best practices programs is integral to their success throughout the organization. One corporate diversity manager for a communication services company said, "He [the CEO] sets the tone for our diversity efforts. He's a diversity champion and speaks of that routinely. He shows support both externally and internally. He expresses his belief that it's a business imperative and not just something nice to do." We'd all like to work for a company like that!

The best companies distinguish themselves from the others in the depth and breadth of their programs. The programs are not independently run by the women employees nor are they part of human resources. Rather, they're incorporated into the overall vision, fabric, and culture of the companies.

Things You Can and Can't Control

If you've decided things are not going well in your career and you need to make a change, it can leave you feeling uncertain and insecure. Be realistic about your future as you take the steps to move forward, and one important element is having an understanding of what you can—and can't—control in the process. For example:

You are in control of . . .

- Keeping up your networking activities
- Acquiring new skills and experience
- Staying current in your field of expertise
- Communicating your goals and experience
- Maintaining your impact and presence
- Refining and enhancing your résumé

You do not have control of . . .

- Your boss
- Your company culture
- The company's financial situation
- Company policies

- Technological changes
- Changing market conditions

If you find the areas where you have no control are problematic for you, you may ultimately need to explore other alternatives. In the meantime, focus on what you *can* control and do your best in those areas.

Tip: Job Security Is the Ability to Find a New Job

These are not the good old days when people routinely stayed in their jobs for decades and retired at the same company where they began their career. If circumstances have decreased your workplace marketability, take steps to remedy the situation so that you can feel more "secure." The new definition of job security is knowing how to find a job when you need one.

Exploring Your Options

The *Three-Minute Recap* is a more specific variation on the drill used in chapter 2, "Make the Connection," where we prepared for formal networking meetings. This drill prepares you for face-to-face meetings with contacts who can help you make connections to a potential job opportunity or new company. The practice you put into these meetings may well determine your future success—so give it your all.

Three-Minute Recap (Example)

Establish Rapport . . . As we discussed over the phone, I'm here today because I've been doing some thinking about my career, and feel that it may be time for me to explore job opportunities outside my present company. Since you are tuned in to the market, I wanted to touch base with you and see if you might have some advice for me. *Note: You're not asking for a job, or even a job lead. Instead, you're asking for advice.*

My Work Experience and Career History . . . We've known each other for a few years, but I thought I would quickly summarize my background for you. I was raised in Buffalo, New York, and came to this area to attend the University of Pennsylvania. I received a bachelor's degree in English and went on to get an MBA in finance at the Wharton School. I was then recruited as a financial analyst by the chemical company, Alston, and gained great skills there. After several years, I realized I wanted to transfer my skills to a company that had a product I could identify with, so I went to Macall, the cosmetics company, where I have risen to the director of finance. Unfortunately, as you may know, Macall has had problems with one of its products and market share has been declining. I'm afraid there will be lay-offs in the near future, so I decided to start looking for a new opportunity. *Note: Hit the highlights of your career history, and include an explanation of why you're looking for a new job.*

My Greatest Strengths and How I've Used Them . . . My greatest strengths are that I love working with numbers, and am good at analyzing and interpreting them. I'm highly organized and self-motivated. I run a five-person department and have been told I'm a good leader—and that my work is done well and on time. Our department is known for coming up with innovative ideas, strategic vision, and follow-through. *Note: In giving your strengths, be confident and reflective—but not cocky.*

My Biggest Accomplishments . . . My biggest accomplishment was researching and contributing the idea for a new type of accounting system, which Macall has adopted. The CEO and CFO were pleased because it made our subsidiary presidents more accountable for budgets, but it also provides significant advantages for the subsidiary presidents like tracking specific costs. *Note: Make this a clear statement of something you did well, with concrete results, and are proud of—let your enthusiasm show.*

What I'm Interested In . . . I'm interested in a company where I can take my finance skills and leadership experience and contribute to the bottom line. I'm particularly interested in a company like Harrington, Inc. but I don't know anyone there. *Note: Be open to suggestions, but have a specific target company in mind you need help with.*

Ask for Advice . . . I wonder if you know anyone at Harrington, Inc. I might speak to, or if you have other ideas about how I might use my skills and who else I might talk to. *Note: Ask for something that's easy to give, so the pressure is off your contact and he or she can settle into "advice-giving" mode.*

Your Time Is Up . . . Now listen for feedback and advice. At the end of the meeting, thank him or her for their time and help.

Conclusion . . . Is there any way I can be of assistance to you? If there is, I hope you'll contact me. Thank you for your time today. I will keep you informed of my progress with the people whose names you've given me. *Note: Offer your contact reciprocity—it is a valuable gift to give—and follow through on keeping your contact informed. Always end the meeting on time.*

Tip: **Keep Your Eye on the Clock**

When you begin a meeting, check how much time you have up front and be aware of how quickly time can go. Make sure, for example, your rapport building doesn't take up the time you need to get your message across. Be sensitive to signals that the other person is ready to end the meeting, such as fidgeting, acting disinterested, or looking at their watch. If you notice these, be ready to end the meeting by making your request for referrals and thanking your contact for the time.

Now, practice using your own situation.

Three-Minute Recap

Establish Rapport . . .

My Work Experience and Career History . . .

My Greatest Strengths and How I've Used Them . . .

My Biggest Accomplishments . . .

What I'm Interested In . . .

Ask for Advice . . .

Your time is up.

Conclusion . . .

Should You Consider Being an Entrepreneur?

Perhaps you've reached a juncture in your career when you're ready for a change, and wonder if that change might involve starting your own business. The Small Business Administration and others have estimated that there are now over 9 million women entrepreneurs, according to the Center for Women's Business Research, 2008.

Why are so many women starting their own businesses? With so many women disillusioned with aspects of the corporate culture, it's not hard to imagine that the frustrations they've experienced have encouraged them to take a new direction, one where they have more independence, flexibility, and control. As a banking executive we surveyed stated, "I had a strong desire to start my own business that would follow my own vision and values." Flexibility was an issue for several women. One woman who left a consulting firm, said, "I know my friends were surprised that I was willing to step off the 'big platform'—no more first-class travel, no more giving speeches. But all that was not at the core of my value system. Now, I have the flexibility I love." Another senior woman at a large retailer who started her own business was delighted with her independence. She said, "I love it. I can apply my corporate skills to develop a business and marketing plan."

If this is something you're seriously considering, read on to see if you have what it takes to be a successful entrepreneur. According a 2002 article in *The Wall Street Journal*, the Small Business Administration forecasts that 63 percent of new businesses will fail within six years. *You* don't want to be a statistic!

Twelve Essentials for Entrepreneurial Success

1. *General Business Experience.* You'll need a basic business background with the understanding of what profit and loss (P&L) statements are and "how money is made."
2. *Specific Knowledge.* Be sure you have a thorough understanding of the business you're entering into. If you're buying a franchise, for example, and don't know the business, make sure you get the support and training you'll need.
3. *Capital or Clients.* Without an immediate source of revenue, your business owner status can be short-lived. Arrange a line of credit or have a couple of clients lined up to start you off.
4. *Competent and Trustworthy Staff.* Hire people who complement the skills you don't possess—for example, if you're the marketing/sales guru,

find a great finance or operations person. Get the best people you can in terms of competencies and trust.

5. *Leadership Skills.* As an entrepreneur, your skills as a leader and decision maker are vital to your success. You'll need to stay the course without being unduly influenced by temporary setbacks or letting others' opinions sway you.

6. *Can-Do Attitude.* Even when you're the head honcho, as an entrepreneur you need to substitute the big corporation attitude with "whatever it takes." As the owner of the business, you'll frequently need to pitch in and do the most basic tasks.

7. *Risk Taking.* Going out on your own is risky and you must be willing to put your time—and perhaps money—on the line with your best effort. If you're truly afraid, or have significant ongoing financial obligations, it probably isn't the right step at this time.

8. *Flexibility.* Market and economic conditions are ever-changing, and as an entrepreneur, you have to monitor them closely and change and adapt your business strategy with them.

9. *Focus.* From the moment you start your business, be focused on the goals you have set and keep them uppermost in your and your employees' minds at all times.

10. *Sales Drive.* It is your job, as business owner, to get out and sell your product or service. You are the primary spokesperson and cheerleader for your company, especially in the beginning. This is key—so if sales scares you, you may need to rethink whether you should be an entrepreneur.

11. *Juggling Delivery and Sales.* One of the toughest parts of starting your own business is managing your sales activity and the delivery of your product or service. The challenge is to keep an eye on both sides of the business—keep your pipeline full of opportunities and the quality of your product high.

12. *Independence.* As tempting as it may be in the short term, resist the urge to bring in partners or investors in order to lighten your load. While it may help you get through a temporary crisis, it's your company and if you give up control early on you may be sorry.

Being an entrepreneur can be lonely. Even the best idea and business plan may not provide the collegiality you had thrived on in your corporation. In fact, many businesses are home-based, especially at the beginning. Some women elect to work at home because it provides the ability to be available for their children. This can lead to even more isolation. It's wise to be aware of this common problem and take steps to counter it.

It is important to continue your networking activities and you may want to enhance them by forming a group of women entrepreneurs who can share similar experiences, thoughts, and ideas. This was done by a group in Philadelphia, who formed a networking club of women entrepreneurs in noncompetitive businesses. They share success strategies, marketing ideas, and even client lists—as well as business leads and introductions. The group has been very successful in its mission, and the women members enjoy each other's support on both a personal and business level.

Planning for Your Future

Just as it is vital for you to plan the next move in your career, it's also important to think about, and plan for, the end of your career and the next stage of your life.

Did you know that every day for the next eighteen years, an estimated five thousand women in the United States will turn 65, according to the Pew Research Center? Unfortunately, the majority are not prepared for the next stage—retirement. Retirement means different things to different people and can happen at almost any age from fifty to eighty. The years when everyone—mostly men—got their gold watches and ceremoniously left the working world at sixty-five, are over. These days not only do people work longer but many want to continue being active even after they leave what they are doing. So a number of retirement-age people don't really retire at all—they just change course.

There are many factors that drive decisions about retirement, including finances, family obligations, personality type, and health. Some people have saved enough to retire completely from the traditional workforce without significantly altering their lifestyles. Many others want or need to continue work, perhaps doing something new and more personally rewarding. My friend Colleen, who started and runs her own company, views work as part of her identity. She often says, "I will die working at my desk. I love what I do and have no intention of retiring." For others, retirement will be dictated by health issues or a need to lessen stress. If you are at the age where you have given thought to retirement—or should!—take the next quiz.

Quiz

When I think about retiring, it is because . . .

- ☐ I am tired
- ☐ I am stressed
- ☐ Work is taking a toll on my health
- ☐ I want to spend more time with friends and family
- ☐ My spouse or partner has recently retired
- ☐ I want to devote more time to a hobby or cause
- ☐ My company has a lucrative retirement package
- ☐ I'd like to relocate to a warmer or different climate
- ☐ I am bored with my job
- ☐ I want to do something incredibly different with my life

Your answers will likely change over time based on changes in your life and thinking, and it's a good idea to periodically quiz yourself to get a reading on your current state of mind.

The ten years prior to the traditional retirement age can be an awfully busy decade. Now, finally, you are a professional in your prime. You have earned that fancy title, and you log long hours to complete demanding work and maintain your edge. You may also be a primary caretaker, tending to the needs of elderly parents while also continuing to financially and emotionally support your teenage or adult children. If your children are out of the house, you might find yourself taking care of grandchildren on the weekends. In fact, research from Prudential Financial indicates that six out of ten retirees are caring for someone in the period five years before or after retirement—and, of course, these care duties tend to fall disproportionately to women.

Maggie is still years away from retirement and fully engaged as an entrepreneur—working happily and diligently as a principal at her consulting firm. Her parents, in their eighties, are becoming increasingly needy in terms of time and attention. Maggie also has three adult children in various stages of their careers, and they frequently need her time and support. Her oldest daughter recently had a baby, and Maggie tries to step in as much as she can to give her daughter a break. Maggie is where many women find themselves, caught in the traditional "sandwich"—the squeeze between elderly parents, children, and now grandchildren. And while Maggie derives an enormous amount of pleasure from most of these activities, they can be exhausting.

Maggie has come to realize that her story is not so different from many other women. She knows too that she needs to give some real thought to her retirement and what will become of her business.

Here's the catch about retirement: it requires your time, energy, and attention while your career and personal life are in full swing. Planning for those years is not as complicated as you might think, however. Given our natural tendencies, we women can have a lot of fun with the retirement planning process. Women, because of the way our brains are configured, tend to move very easily between the left side and the right side of the brain when approaching almost any problem, often employing both a creative and a practical point of view. Simply stated, women can use their right and left brain simultaneously when addressing a task or solving a problem. As a result, women often see a problem and its solution from multiple perspectives. Women can combine the desire to create a retirement scenario that draws upon their most heartfelt dreams and aspirations yet still be practical and realistic.

Tip: Don't Forget Your Partner

In retirement planning, there is usually, though not always, a partner or spouse in the picture. Bringing your partner into this process might give you some additional insights and result in a plan that works well for both of you. The subject for that conversation is, "What does retirement look like to me?" Choose a good time for both of you, sit down, and share your thoughts.

As you contemplate your choices for the future, it may be helpful to think about people you know who have retired and how, in each case, retirement has worked out for them. Here are some suggestions about questions to research.

- Do you know someone who retired and took on a second career entirely different from his or her prior work life?
- Do you know people who dramatically changed their style of living—where they lived, their relationship with family and friends, their basic life priorities?
- Do you know of anyone whose health improved once he or she retired—or, conversely, who suffered health problems due to the stresses related to retirement?

- Do you know of anyone whose marriage or family relationships improved—or not—after retirement?
- What about someone who chose to volunteer her time in retirement?

Doing some thinking and exploring can help you gain insight into what makes retirement successful—or unsuccessful. Whose has been the most successful retirement you know? What makes it successful in your eyes? Why? Whose has been the least successful? Why?

Unfortunately, we hear a lot of stories about individuals whose retirement has not turned out the way they envisioned it. We can learn much by thinking about the experiences of others and applying them to ourselves. By being thoughtful about the issues and, in essence, managing the process of your retirement, you greatly increase the opportunity to spend your retirement days in a very positive and satisfying place.

As you plan your retirement activities, the skills we have covered in this book—building relationships, assessing your skills, communicating effectively and selling your strengths will help you as you consider your retirement options. Whether you choose consulting, part-time work, a new career, or more unstructured time, taking the time to evaluate and strategize your choices will give you the best chance of a happy retirement

9

Special for Women of African Descent
Leveling the Playing Field

The most successful women of African descent seem to be able to turn the concept of being a "double outsider" to their advantage. They possess extra measures of strength, resilience, and grace that set them apart. It's an extraordinary capacity that they are able to tap into in order to move ahead.

—Deborah E. Brown, adjunct professor, diversity, New York University

IN ORDER TO better understand the issues, similarities, and differences of Caucasian women and women of African descent in the workplace, The Leader's Edge/Leaders By Design brought together women of different races from corporations throughout the greater Philadelphia area. Each woman invited was asked to bring a guest of the opposite race. The goal was for the women to brainstorm the biggest issues dividing them and suggest solutions for how they might bridge the gaps between them. A number of focus groups and interviews led by The Leader's Edge/Leaders By Design, and our collective experience coaching women of all backgrounds, had indicated a lack of understanding by each group about the issues of the other.

Most of the white women polled had never had the opportunity for open and honest discussion about race with women of another race, and perhaps had never thought about the differences in their backgrounds, experiences, and more important, the barriers they face because of the color of their skin. The black women we spoke with saw this as insensitivity, and it felt to them that important issues were being "swept under the rug" instead of getting the attention and thought they deserved.

In fact, it is not always the obvious things that create barriers for women of African descent. Small slights, micro-inequities, and subtle omissions can add up over time, taking a tremendous toll on performance, eroding confidence, and producing a lack of trust.

This discussion represented new and uncharted territory for many participants, and yielded a number of suggestions. Many said that it is important to challenge assumptions and to reach out to others by starting a dialogue—even if it involves stepping out of your comfort zone. A number of the women stated that it is important to take the risk with each other to be more open and honest. This, they felt, is necessary to developing trust. They all agreed that in the end, when a woman advances, no matter what color she is, it is a success for all women.

In this chapter, we take this advice to heart by raising issues often ignored because they may be uncomfortable—or they are just not often discussed. We believe it is important to talk about the unique issues and challenges faced daily by women of African descent as they navigate through the workplace because, in addition to the myriad of difficulties encountered as women, they have a second set of obstacles due to their skin color. They often tell us that they struggle with a number of questions. *How do I get people to overcome biases, and to accept me and acknowledge my abilities? What do I need to do to be considered for leadership positions and the development programs offered to individuals believed to have high potential? How can I establish a greater comfort level with the managers and executives who determine my advancement?* And, all too often, African American women say their response to the barriers they face is to close up and stop communicating, and that they have nobody to turn to for answers to the many questions about their careers with which they struggle.

According to a 2004 survey on Advancing African American Women in the Workplace by the Catalyst organization, the percentage of corporate officers in the Fortune 500 companies who are African American women is only 1.1 percent. African American women report that their authority and credibility are often questioned, and that other work challenges include lack of consistent company support, stereotyping, and exclusion from informal networks. This chapter supplements the subjects covered in the rest of this book and discusses the unique challenges of women of African descent in terms of communication, visibility, mentoring, and developing networks, offering practical advice in these important areas. We also suggest ways in which women of all backgrounds can be stronger allies and partners, and support each other's success.

Tip: Empower Yourself

There is no doubt that life—and work—should be fairer and there should be fewer biases. But, much of the insensitivity and inequity you experience is done without conscious thought or malice. Instead of letting it get to you, think about what you can do to address issues, head them off, and level the playing field. This way, you are not giving others the power to diminish your confidence.

Taking on a Leadership Role

Given the many roadblocks encountered by women of African descent, it is not difficult to understand why uncertainty exists for many about how their company or organization views them in terms of advancement, and where they fit as leadership candidates. Further, unless they have a strong support base, they may be uncomfortable about asking for the professional development and other resources needed to take on greater responsibility. And, frequently, managers are fearful of giving feedback that may be taken the wrong way. Therefore, it is crucial for African American women to ask for the feedback they need and be open to receiving advice.

Take this quiz to see if you are on track for leadership in your organization.

Are you on track for leadership roles?	*Yes*	*No*
1. Have you indicated an interest in advancing to your human resources and your boss?	☐	☐
2. Have you sought and received feedback on your professional style and your work?	☐	☐
3. Have you been open to feedback you've received?	☐	☐
4. Do you volunteer for high-visibility projects and initiatives?	☐	☐

5. Are you viewed as someone with goals and potential? ☐ ☐
6. Are you aware of your areas for improvement? ☐ ☐
7. Have you ever applied for higher level positions? ☐ ☐
8. Do you know the reasons you did or did not receive
   past promotions? ☐ ☐
9. Do you understand your skills, strengths, and gaps? ☐ ☐

If you have zero to three nos, it sounds like you are ready to advance in your career while you work on the areas for improvement. If you have four or more nos, you'll want to reassess the steps you are taking toward leadership. You may find that you need to be more self-aware and goal-oriented. Focus on assessing yourself in light of your career goals, and take the necessary steps toward success.

As you are considering where you fit in as a leader, it is important to take stock of what you bring to the opportunities open in your organization, and what skill gaps you may need to fill to achieve your goals. In thinking about your skills, experience, and accomplishments, don't forget to include the "personal" side of your life. If you have experience leading projects in your community, for example, take a good look at how that transfers to the workplace. In many cases, you will find that the nontraditional ways in which you have gained skills, such as volunteer work, leadership in your church, and even family roles, are valuable and transferable assets when effectively combined with more traditional training. The challenge is to define these skills, and then to be able to articulate them in a way that conveys their importance and relevance.

Teresa was very interested in getting ahead at her company, and routinely reviewed the internal job postings looking for a good fit. When she came across a position in the human resources department's benefits area, she was excited and immediately started matching her skills to the job requirements. She noted two areas of possible concern. The first was the specification for "two to five years' experience managing people," and the second was a requirement for a master's degree. Teresa's first reaction was that she just didn't have the qualifications for the job and wouldn't even apply. However, upon reflection, she realized she needed to do some thinking outside the box. Though in her present position she didn't have people reporting to her, she did manage people in her role as advisory board member and head of the volunteer committee at her daughter's school. Moreover, she realized that managing volunteers requires real finesse—and she'd even won an award for her effort. As far as the advanced degree, though Teresa didn't have one, she was taking her second evening course working toward her master's degree, and was getting excellent grades. She decided to apply for the HR position—presenting her qualifications in a positive manner and showing how they applied to the listing. She received an interview and got the job.

Tip: Ask for Help from the Right People

Don't expect others to come to you to present an opportunity. Instead, once you have established the goal of getting more responsibility and a higher title, take the initiative to go to the right person in your organization and discuss your career goals. Before you meet, make certain you understand the training and development resources available in your company. Be ready to link your goals and skills with the courses, coaching, or training that will enable you to be a better performer and leader—and ask for help. Make sure you talk about how the company will benefit from your new knowledge!

Communication

As we know, there are vast differences between women and men in the important area of communication. As their styles collide, it is often difficult for the women to get their viewpoints heard and valued by men. Because white males have traditionally dictated the "norms," many business cultures still carry their imprint and, until there are more women, we need to consider this as we develop our individual styles.

These same challenges arise for many women of African descent, who find that their approach differs not only from the men they work with, but from their white women colleagues as well. Many times, Caucasian women are socialized to be "good girls" who take pains to be agreeable and avoid conflict, even in the business environment. Women of African descent often feel uncomfortable with what they see as a façade which clashes with their more frank and expressive style of communication.

Women of African descent, even highly educated and experienced executives, often feel that they must be extra careful about what they say and how they say it. As members of a very small minority, they know the scrutiny they are under. This can lead to trying to reach an unrealistic standard of perfection and being overly fearful of making a mistake. While being knowledgeable and prepared is important, we have seen women stopped in their tracks when questioned or challenged because they want to make sure their response is "perfect."

Another issue encountered by black women is how the tone of their message is interpreted by others. One woman put it this way: "What I say gets perceived differently. If I'm strong in my opinion, I'm seen as too aggressive or disrespectful. When a white woman says the same thing she is considered great." Ironically, this is the same thing that white women often say about men. There is clearly a narrow band of communication style perceived to be appropriate for all women—and it gets even narrower for women of African descent.

Tip: **Get a Second Opinion**

If you've gotten the vibe—either directly or indirectly—that your communication style is putting off your colleagues, get an honest opinion from someone else. Is there an individual you trust who can give you the feedback you need—and keep it confidential? He or she, black or white, could be a coworker, a human resources person, or a friend at another company. Be sure to ask the right questions in order to get the feedback you need!

Since communication style is key to getting your message across, it is clear that in order to be heard and get credit for their good ideas, women should do the necessary preparation for meetings in order to be confident in their knowledge. This includes having an understanding of their colleagues, whose support and respect is crucial to a positive outcome. Women also must take steps to understand and assess their delivery and its impact in order to make necessary adjustments to engage their audience.

Take this quiz to gauge if your workplace communication style holds you back. Be honest with yourself!

Is your communication style holding you back?	*Yes*	*No*
1. Do you sense that others are put off by your communication style?	☐	☐
2. Are you frequently told by colleagues that your communication style is too aggressive?	☐	☐

3. Do others say the same thing as you do, but get the credit?   ☐   ☐

4. Do you refrain from speaking if you don't have all the answers?   ☐   ☐

5. Do you usually avoid speaking to colleagues you don't know?   ☐   ☐

6. Do you hoard information rather than share with colleagues?   ☐   ☐

7. Do you often take others by surprise by presenting ideas they haven't heard before?   ☐   ☐

If you have two or fewer yeses, it sounds like you are on target with your communication style. If you have three or more yeses, you'll want to reassess the way in which you are delivering your message in the workplace. Your style may be holding you back from being heard, getting credit for your ideas, and ultimately, getting ahead.

Networking

Building a powerful network and a strong base of influential allies is something that can seem like an overwhelming challenge to women of African descent, many of whom express feelings of isolation and exclusion in business environments. Though it requires a great deal of work, by creating a diverse and open business network you are able to access opportunities otherwise overlooked.

Tip: Connect with Colleagues

It is smart to reach out to develop pleasant relationships with colleagues of both genders and all races, and to occasionally participate in lunch gatherings, after-work coffee, or drinks. Though this requires time and effort, the pay-off is your inclusion in the all-important informal information loop. Don't worry about becoming BFFs with your coworkers. You can keep it cordial, productive, and professional without spending time together outside of work. Remember, you are expanding your network—not necessarily creating social friendships.

Since creating a network of support at work is an important element in getting ahead, keep in mind that though it often seems like you are the only one who feels like an outsider, there are many women and men around you who are also striving to be liked and respected by colleagues—and it may feel just as uncomfortable to them.

Joelle always felt a little uneasy when she represented her department at the monthly meeting. Since she didn't really know the other participants, she often arrived late to avoid the awkwardness of having to make conversation. The few times she tried to contribute to the discussion, she felt invisible—it seemed as if no one heard her.

When she arrived at the February meeting at her usual time, she found that they had decided to wait for a few people who had been caught in a traffic jam. As Joelle sat down and prepared to look through her notes, a woman took the seat next to her, put out her hand and said, "Hi, I'm Kim Davis from accounting. This is my first time at this meeting." Joelle introduced herself—with some initial reluctance—and filled Kim in on the agenda. Soon, their conversation was joined by the man sitting on Joelle's left, who was replacing his vacationing colleague at the meeting. By the time the meeting got under way, the discussion was animated, and when Joelle later presented an idea to the group, it was met with enthusiasm. Joelle realized that knowing her colleagues helped her find her voice because she felt much more a part of the group. She resolved that in the future she would make more of an effort to get to know her colleagues.

The first step in developing your network is to assess the dynamics of those around you. Who seems to have solid relationships with a broad spectrum of people? Which individuals do you admire? Who has been helpful to you and seems open to more of a relationship? What are their objectives—are they compatible with yours? Start slowly and make connections one at a time. As you uncover common interests and philosophies, you may also discover that your colleagues know people you don't to whom you can be introduced and with whom you can build relationships. One by one, you can extend your network over time, with people who are receptive, in a way that is comfortable for you. Look for opportunities to assist colleagues by introducing them to new people, too. This helps create more allies for you and a climate of mutual support that will help in your endeavors.

How Diverse Is Your Network?

Take a look at the people in your life whom you see on a social, rather than strictly business, basis. Think of people you spend time with having lunch, talking informally, in a group after work, or driving with/walking to meetings. Consider your work colleagues, outside business associates, and members of organizations you belong to. Mark an X for each individual you know in each category to see how diverse—or not—your network really is. Mark an X in the appropriate section of the following chart for each person in your business-related network.

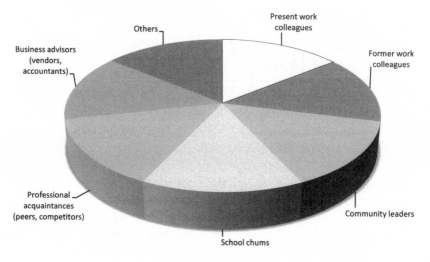

Now, go back and circle each X representing a person of another gender, race, or nationality, and then ask yourself:

- Are you surprised by the results of your chart?
- Does your network include people of different genders and races?
- Is it global in nature?
- Would it be helpful to make an effort to include different types of people as you broaden your network?

While reaching out is always a risk, by staying within a "safe" environment of people you already know and feel comfortable with—or going it alone—you are limiting your horizons in your organization and perhaps your career. One woman spoke of this as "self-exclusion." Keep in mind that social dynamics in the workplace are always tricky, and it is wise to emphasize areas of common ground rather than dwelling on differences. One important area of commonality may well be that you both want to get ahead and can help each other reach that goal. Other common areas may be that you are working mothers, that you are women in a man's world, or that you are both trying to balance work and life.

Promoting Yourself

An African American woman in one of the focus groups told us, "I know I have to self-promote for people to see what I have done. Growing up, my dad used to tell us 'Your work speaks for itself'—but, unfortunately, those words don't apply now." How right she is! Though many women have been given this same message, as you move up the ladder you need to promote yourself and your work in order to get ahead.

To gain credibility, and not allow people to underestimate what you have to offer, it is essential to tell them about your skills, experience, and accomplishments. And, by giving them information about you, your projects, and your capabilities, you will impede them from putting you into a category based on ignorance and stereotyping. As we talked about in our earlier chapter on self-promotion, you will need to dig deep and think through the questions:

- What do you want to be known for?
- What are your top accomplishments?
- What is unique about your skills?
- What have you done to demonstrate leadership?
- What special value do you provide to your teams and organization?

By exploring and understanding the answers to these and other questions, you will develop the confidence and focus to tell others about yourself and enlist their support in accomplishing the goals you have set. A confident person who can articulate her contributions attracts others to her!

Organizational Savvy

Assessing your organization, its culture, and the way in which decisions are made is necessary and an ongoing responsibility for anyone who wants to get ahead. In order to get the information so vital to your career, it is important to get to know people in different areas of your company, as well as those on the outside—competitors, business advisors, and other professionals.

How can you get the diverse perspectives and information you need?

- Schedule lunches/coffee with a variety of colleagues and associates.
- Attend functions of your department or company and chat it up with people.
- Keep your eyes open for seminars and networking events that are on-topic and will likely garner an interesting audience.
- Roam the halls occasionally and drop in to say hello to people.
- Regularly schedule one-on-one meetings to update your boss.
- E-mail good ideas and articles to key decision makers.
- Take courses that will build your résumé and put you in the path of other ambitious individuals.

When she started work at the new firm, Bonnie found that she knew one of her colleagues through their church. As the "new kid," Bonnie was relieved when Carol invited her to join her lunch group—and she gladly accepted. The group consisted of three other women of color who worked in Carol's department, and had been at the company for years. Bonnie had a lot in common with all the women, who had lunch together almost daily and saw each other frequently outside of work. While she felt comfortable with her lunch pals, she began to notice that several men and women in her department had lunch with their boss occasionally. When she said something to one of her coworkers about being included, the response was that she would be welcome to come, but hadn't been asked because she always seemed to have plans. Only then did Bonnie realize that she may have been isolating herself by sticking so closely to her lunch group. Though she and her lunch buddies had become friends, if she wanted to develop more and better relationships, and get in the loop on company information, she would be smart to vary her lunchtime routine. The next time the group started to gather, she asked to join them and immediately received an enthusiastic response.

Is your comfortable routine unintentionally creating a barrier for interaction with others? Are you missing out on viewpoints and information by sticking to a "clique"? Take an objective look at your activities and actions, and see if there are opportunities you are missing. By making a few minor changes, you may be able to gain a significant advantage.

Tip: Run Faster, Be Sharper

Climbing the organizational ladder is not for the faint of heart. Understand that you will have to deal with misconceptions about you, that there will be fewer trailblazers ahead of you, and that you will get less support than you would like. Yet, in the face of all that, if you want to win you must stay in the game, demonstrate that you are good, and keep setting the bar high. According to a very successful African American woman leader, you also have to be "faster, smarter, and sharper."

Finding a Mentor

"Along the way at these corners that you turn in life, there are people, if you're fortunate, who can nudge you in a direction, or urge you to be courageous, and that, to me, is the essence of what mentoring is," says journalist Gwen Ifill.

Many senior women leaders are in demand as mentors—and that goes double for women leaders of African descent, who are in such short supply that they are often stretched to the limit. Yet, it is vital to be mentored—and the good news is that great mentors, who can make a big difference in your career success, can be people of either gender and any color.

One woman of color said, "I had three people who could help me in different ways: a white woman who was my peer, a black woman who was in senior management, and a white male who was my manager. All three were a huge help to me." The key is to match your mentoring needs carefully with the individuals available to you.

Consider people who value diversity, understand its many benefits, and have a demonstrated commitment. Reflect on leaders within your organization as well as those outside. Don't forget to include community leaders who, depending on your needs, may prove to be excellent mentors.

And, if you are currently in a position of leadership, it is important for you to model behavior for those who are coming up in the ranks, and to be available as a mentor to other women of color.

Developing Impact and Presence

When discussing the subject of women and leadership presence, one woman of African descent spoke about the need to have a high confidence level to get ahead. She said, "It's a matter of degree that makes the difference between what white women and black women experience. Black women are more self-conscious about appearance because there's more at stake for us. We feel that everything we do adds to the judgment people form."

It often seems that the light shines brightly on everything that's said and done by successful women in the workplace because there are so few.

This can be a daily challenge requiring a big dose of self-confidence. Unfortunately, there are only a small number of senior women—and still fewer who are African American—to serve as role models for more junior women. Black women have mentioned an important issue—that of feeling like they are being labeled by white coworkers who, in attempting to understand where their black colleagues "fit," frequently try to put them into a category. One senior-level black woman says that when she walks into a meeting, she sometimes feels she's being labeled as one of three stereotypes: "provocative," "subservient," or "overly aggressive." This is likely caused by misinformation and misunderstanding about their African American colleagues. For example, if a black woman brings a significantly different background and set of experiences into the workplace, her perspective and outlook may vary from those of others. This fresh viewpoint and diverse thinking should be valued, not feared. As white colleagues—especially other women—show more support to their black female associates, over time this situation can change for the better.

What Can You Do about These Issues?

Understand who you are, what you represent, and that you may be different from most of your colleagues. Then—be at ease with this, and go about your work with dignity instead of allowing it to become a distraction.

Tip: Organizational Cultures Trump Fashion Trends

If your goal is to get ahead in your company or organization, you will likely have to save the strong fashion statement for your personal life. Since organizations have distinct cultural parameters in terms of image and don't usually encourage extreme deviations, be sure to adapt your style to be consistent with your environment. Understand the issues—then make an informed choice about how you present yourself.

Janet and Debbie rarely had the opportunity to meet for lunch, so the two friends greeted each other enthusiastically when they arrived at the café. As they detached from their embrace, Debbie said, "Wow, we rarely get to see each other during the workday. This is great!" As they sat down, she added, "Your company doesn't mind if you dress that way?" Janet looked surprised—then quickly scanned Debbie's flattering jacket and understated accessories. She realized her outfit was pretty bold by comparison with her flowing shawl, long skirt, and striking earrings. She paused a moment, then said, "Well, you know how I like to make a statement. But honestly, I never gave much thought to how the people I work with view it." As they ate, Debbie talked about her philosophy of "dressing for success," which she felt was extremely important for women and minorities. Their discussion prompted Janet to think about whether her appearance might be holding her back. She realized the leaders in her organization dressed more like Janet, and that if she toned down her daytime style, it would be more in tune with the culture. She asked Janet to go shopping with her, and the next time the two met for lunch, Debbie admired Janet's new, more professional look.

As you are fine-tuning a personal brand that's right for you, think about the following questions:

- How do company decision makers view you in terms of image, impact, and presence?
- Does your appearance always stand out in a group? Do you believe this has helped or hurt your career?
- Have you assessed your style to see if it's on target? Have you received feedback from others?
- Are you able to maintain your individuality while staying in tune with your organization?

The bottom line is—are you comfortable with the image you are projecting? Is it helping you achieve your goals? If not, seek the assistance you need to create an image that works for you. Get feedback, be observant, find a personal shopper or a friend who has a good style sense. Taking action will put you on track for your career goals instead of allowing this issue to get in the way of your success.

Taking Control of Your Career

"You have to be true to yourself and enjoy what you're doing. That's what gets you through difficult times. Set goals, stick to them, and don't get bogged down with 'scorecarding' yourself on every little detail. Instead, keep your eye on the prize."

This wisdom comes from a woman of color who is a leader at a prominent Fortune 100 company. And she's right on target. In order to move ahead in your career, it is critical to know what your goals are, and to keep moving toward them in spite of the obstacles and barriers you may encounter. Ultimately, your success requires tenacity to see the path ahead rather than dwelling on opportunities lost.

"I noticed that various kinds of leadership development and training were routinely offered to others—but never to me," lamented a black woman in one of our focus sessions. It is easy to see how she might feel left out and ignored. But, instead of getting discouraged, the way to turn it around is to step up and ask for training, development, and feedback. In fact, many black women are not routinely tapped for training, and many of the women who go through The Leader's Edge/Leaders By Design coaching and training programs tell us that this is the *first* significant leadership training in which they have participated—and all of them had to *ask*!

We have noticed, too, that the women who go through our program often do not hold titles commensurate with their skills and experience. Compared with their white female colleagues, African American women need to be attentive to this issue, and to question something if it appears imbalanced. When you do this, be sure you have all the facts and present your case to the right people, in the right way. Once you gather some information and approach your boss, you'll want to be sure it's a good time to initiate a conversation about the topic. Then you might say, "I have just completed the XYZ project successfully after launching the ABC project ahead of schedule. Is there anything else I need to do to be considered for a promotion?" The idea is to recruit your boss as an ally who wants to assist you.

Tip: Close the Real or Perceived Gaps!

Examine your qualifications and career goals to see if there are areas of experience or education that could hold you back. Whether the gaps are "real" or "perceived," don't give people a reason to deny you a promotion, title, or transfer. Instead, take a hard look at any possible areas that need to be filled, and get the required degree, training, or experience before it becomes an obstacle to advancement.

At this time in history, many factors, including a talent shortage, changing demographics, and a global economy, have caused companies to put greater value on diversity. As companies begin to evolve from their embedded cultures, it is a good time to be a woman of African descent trying to get ahead and take on a leadership role. Remember, your talents are needed and you deserve to have the chance to reach your goals, though it will take time for organizations to truly understand more about you and the value you bring.

Tip: By Sharing We Learn to Trust

It takes guts to reach out and start a dialogue with someone new, but though you may feel vulnerable, it is an important step toward mutual understanding. By sharing a little piece of yourself you are, in effect, educating your colleague about who you are and what you bring to the table. It is likely that she or he will want to continue the conversation, giving you the opportunity to learn more about her. Only through this sharing will you be able to trust and support each other.

If you sense that you are being wrongly judged by a colleague, consider opening a conversation with the purpose of tactfully informing and educating her about who you are and the experiences that have shaped you. If your colleague is open-minded and has good intentions, she will be happy to feel more enlightened. Unless there is more understanding and a deeper appreciation among women, nothing will change.

Some thoughts to keep in mind . . .

- Don't be limited by your vision.
- Expect to be viewed and treated differently.
- Be proud of your difference.
- Push back on stereotyping.
- Build allies.
- Look inside yourself and ask the hard questions.
- Hang in there!

Though it sometimes feels lonely, you are not alone in your endeavors. As more and more women rise up the ranks, it is our hope that they will put the energy into developing relationships and giving each other the support they need to get ahead.

The Future
A Third Face of Leadership

ODAY, THERE are two distinctly different faces of leadership in most organizations. These faces are defined by gender—and the male approach was virtually alone until the last few decades, when women entered into leadership roles. Although the two have coexisted, one side ultimately tries to dominate the other and it is usually the men's side that wins. When this happens, women often lose out in their efforts to advance—and the organization is confined to using only half of its available talent. If men and women were able to blend the best of their natural styles, they would be more effective, productive, and ultimately, more successful.

Today, however, organizations have not tapped into the full value of women as leaders in the workplace. Our research shows that of the seven interpersonal leadership skills, women excel in: listening, empathizing, attending, ethical analysis, and maintaining respect in conflict, while men stand out in decision making and speaking with authority. The many differences between the sexes, shown in the next chart, hold the possibility of creating positive dynamics in the work culture—if and when they are combined. This is because the strengths and weaknesses of men and women can often offset each other, producing a stronger, more balanced approach.

Though there are exceptions, many people tend to fall into gender-specific behavior patterns. In order to be most powerful, we propose that

Different Workplace Styles of Men and Women

Men	Women
Control emotions/feelings	Have empathy for others
Excel at short-term decision making	Interested in long-term consequences of decisions
Want to win over others at all costs	Want to succeed with others
Concerned with self-interest	Concerned with needs/wants of others
Treat people impersonally	Have sensitivity to others' feelings/thoughts
Seek and use power	Minimize the need to use power
Hold information close to the vest	Share information with others
Rely on organizational chart	Use collaboration
Confront conflict directly and aggressively	Avoid conflict, look for inclusion
Communicate concisely	Speak comprehensively

the skills and strengths of women and men should be combined into what we call "the third face of leadership," the key principles of which are:

- Seek to acknowledge differences in the styles of men and women, and put the value of each into a professional context
- Incorporate short- and long-term vision and their consequences into their actions
- Balance their needs/wants with those of others and demonstrate regard for individuals
- Deal respectfully with conflicts and look for resolution
- Connect with others through positive, strategic communication and consider what and how information is being exchanged

Third-face leadership is a dramatic change to the predominant leadership approach in today's business environments, and will need time and energy to advance. This can be a lonely endeavor and involves patience, as others begin to learn this new way of viewing colleagues and thinking about leadership. There are still deep-seated biases and ingrained inertia in today's male-dominated cultures, and a shift involves changing the paradigm. However, there are many positive outcomes to be gained through this change:

- *Greater success in the personal growth and development* of leaders who understand the issues of gender and have respect for each other's value.
- *Increased productivity in organizations* by decreasing the tension between genders, and by encouraging women and men to use the many different leadership qualities they naturally bring to the workplace.
- *More understanding,* on the part of men, as to what women bring to leadership positions—and vice versa thereby expanding their range as leaders.
- *A healthier balance* between family and work as the perspective and the priorities of both men and women are included in setting policy at the top of their companies.
- *Fewer ethical scandals* in corporations when both men and women are leaders in top companies. (Remember, many of the whistle-blowers in this decade's most prominent corporate scandals were women!)
- *Long-term profitability* in companies in which men and women lead together. A higher return on equity has been shown in companies with a higher proportion of women.

Finally . . . The common themes for success in all of the strategies we have covered in this book—relationship building, self-promotion, communication, mentoring, presence, political savvy, community involvement, balance, and career change—are *self-awareness* and *planning.* Look at yourself realistically in the context of the corporate landscape and develop an awareness of the areas where you need to continue your growth. Understand the contrasts between you and your male colleagues, and consider how to make them work for you. Think about this book as your personal guide to helping you maximize your contributions as a leader in your organization.

Success is difficult to achieve and requires hard work. Thought and preparation are necessary for success in your current organization—or in the event that you decide to go elsewhere. To succeed, you must know what you want and determine how to get there. Take a hard look at yourself to understand your strengths as a woman, and the obstacles that may be in your way—both small and large—and concentrate on these. To stay on top of your game, and attain what you really want, you must make this process ongoing.

Until more women advance or stay in the top ranks of management, and change the culture of companies, being a woman executive will continue to be difficult and frustrating. If women don't adopt new and different tools, not just to survive, but to shine, the numbers won't change. But if they learn skills and strategies to get their voices heard, communicate without confusion, put themselves on the receiving end of news and information, they will *swing open the boys' club door and participate with full membership.* It is our hope that you find the advice in this book helpful to you in reaching *your* career goals and that once you reach the top, you will lend a hand to the women coming up behind you.

A Man's Perspective
Men Must Be Part of the Solution, Not the Problem

Peter J. Dean, PhD

DEEP INSIDE most men is an innate desire to accomplish something great in some way. Men are programmed from early on to seek being the great achiever, the great athlete, or at least to be great at something. According to Helen Fisher in her 2000 book, *The First Sex: The Natural Talents of Women and How They Are Changing the World*, men have an intense drive and ambition to succeed and can focus their attention to do so. This drive in men is often observed as an ambition to win *over* others. Women want to win, too, but to win *with* others. In order to win, women use their talent for work; capacity to read postures, gestures, and facial expressions; capacity for empathy and emotional sensitivity; penchant for long-term planning; and preference for cooperating and collaborating with others.

In contrast, the predisposition of men to win over is so strong that they often overlook the leadership ability of women and their potential to make important contributions to organizations. Often, for men, their pursuit of greatness gives them an inflated sense of power which brings out a no-holds-barred sense of competition and undermines the efforts of others, especially women.

Men compete with other men in many ways in order to move in the direction of greatness. Sometimes that energy is misdirected.

I worked with a CEO who was passionate about competition with a few CEOs in other firms. They focused their competitive drive on their collections of wooden decoy ducks used in duck hunting. These men seemed to gauge their greatness by tallying the number of wooden ducks held by each. They used to joke, "He who has the most ducks when he dies, wins." These men were accomplished, wealthy, and by all rights, successful in the workplace yet they still seemed to have a need to be seen as great, and it had to be visible enough for everyone else to see.

Men are designed to be competitive—it is literally part of our DNA. And we bring all of that hardwiring and practice to the job. They are physical, loud, and use aggressive nonverbal signals to influence people. James Hillman, in his book *Kinds of Power: A Guide to Its Intelligent Uses*, suggests that the loud "alpha male" behavior has value in competitive environments but may be limited in adding value at other times.

In fact, many men will make visible their competitive urges with power plays, ego-dominated words, loudness, banging on tables, pointing fingers, or other aggressive actions. When men display this type of behavior with other men it's boorish. When it's done around a conference table of men *and* women, a tense work culture is created. These types of behavior are generally distasteful to women, who don't have an understanding of, or affinity for, the aggressive alpha male rules of engagement. Women, instead, draw upon the other ways of leading.

One measure of worth that is vital to most men is the approval of others. Men expect that approval of their deeds should come from others, but oddly enough, men don't generally give the approval they themselves seek. I remember one of my male mentors saying, "If I'm not complaining about your performance, then you know you're doing a good job." He expected me to be satisfied with this. In reality, men are uncomfortable giving positive feedback, so they disguise it or neglect to give it at all. Women, on the other hand, value and need feedback and recognition. This clash of needs and wants creates a chasm between the two genders.

Men need to modify their thoughts and behavior in order to make the workplace a pleasant and productive environment in which both genders make their contributions. In order to improve the work environment, men need to:

- Develop additional skills in their leadership repertoire, including: listening and processing, empathizing with the other person's emotions and feelings, attending to the needs of others, and responding with respect in honest two-way conversation.
- Recognize that women are in the workplace to stay and that men need to lose their misgivings about women. Many men have a predisposition to resist a woman as the leader and consider the woman as not "having what it takes." While some of the team camaraderie with other men may be lost in today's mixed-gender workplace, a new dynamic which is favorable to all will be created.
- Avoid the misuse and overuse of the power of their positions. Generally, men gain power from the prestige of their positions and use it to exercise control. Women are more apt to view power as the ability to influence, and they are often willing to share to accomplish a goal. This different way of using power should be seen as an advantage for the organization.
- Relearn how to communicate with women at work. By understanding the differences in their styles, men will be able to learn how to communicate with women in a way that avoids misunderstandings and increases productivity for both.
- Understand the issues and challenges women encounter due to traditional male-dominated cultures and styles. Be part of the solution, not the problem.

On an ending note, a woman friend who is in a top corporate position shared her views on the subject of men, women, and the achievement of success. She said:

> To be successful, a woman must be perceived as both a "good woman" (wife, mother, daughter, etc.) *and* a good businessperson. There are many reasons we lose women on the way to the top. Some opt to stay home with children, some don't have the goal of a top slot, and some have that goal but refuse to do what they need to in order to get there. This occurs for many different reasons, but mostly, *it is because men seldom understand what a woman brings to the workplace.*

If men are not part of the solution, they may be part of the problem.

Further Reading

Austin, Linda S. *What's Holding You Back? 8 Critical Choices for Women's Success.* New York: Perseus, 2001.

Babcock, Linda. *Women Don't Ask: Negotiation and the Gender Divide.* Princeton, NJ: Princeton University Press, 2003.

Baker, Wayne. *Achieving Success through Social Capital.* San Francisco: Jossey-Bass, 2000.

Barnett, Rosalind. *Same Difference: How the Gender Myths Are Hurting Our Relationships, Our Children, and Our Jobs.* New York: Perseus, 2004.

Bates, Karen Grigsby, and Karen Elyse Hudson. *Basic Black: Home Training for Modern Times.* New York: Broadway, 2002.

Bell, Ella L., and Stella Nkomo. *Our Separate Ways: Black and White Women and the Struggle for Professional Identity.* Boston: Harvard Business School Press, 2003.

Bennis, Warren. *On Becoming a Leader.* New York: Perseus, 1994.

Benton, D. A. *Executive Charisma: Six Steps to Mastering the Art of Leadership.* New York: McGraw-Hill, 2003.

———. *Lions Don't Need to Roar: Using the Leadership Power of Personal Presence to Stand Out, Fit in, and Move Ahead.* New York: Time Warner, 1993.

Betof, Edward, and Nila Betof. *Just Promoted!: A 12-Month Road Map for Success in Your New Leadership Role.* New York: McGraw-Hill, 2010.

Bjorseth, Lillian. *Breakthrough Networking: Building Relationships That Last.* Lisle, IL: Duoforce Enterprises, 1996.

Blum, Arlene. *Annapurna, A Woman's Place.* San Francisco: Sierra Club Books, 1998.

Book, Esther Wachs. *Why the Best Man for the Job Is a Woman.* New York: HarperCollins, 2000.

Brandon, Rick, and Marty Seldman. *Survival of the Savvy: High-Integrity Political Tactics for Career and Company Success.* New York: Free Press, 2004.

Branson, Douglas M. *No Seat at the Table: How Corporate Governance Keeps Women Out of America's Boardrooms.* New York: New York University Press, 2006.

Brizendine, Louann. *The Female Brain.* Three Rivers Press, 2007.

———. *The Male Brain.* Three Rivers Press, 2011.

Carli, Linda, and Alice Eagly. *Through the Labyrinth: The Truth about How Women Become Leaders.* Boston: Harvard Business School Press, 2007.

Charan, Ram. *What the CEO Wants You to Know: How Your Company Really Works.* New York: Crown, 2001.

Ciampa, Dan, and Michael Watkins. *Right from the Start: Taking Charge in a New Leadership Role.* Boston: Harvard Business School Press, 1999.

Cornelius, Helena. *Gentle Revolution: Men and Women at Work: What Goes Wrong and How to Fix It.* Simon & Schuster Australia, 2000.

D'Alessandro, David F. *Career Warfare: 10 Rules for Building a Successful Brand and Fighting to Keep It.* New York: McGraw-Hill, 2004.

Dean, Peter J. *Leadership for Everyone.* New York: McGraw-Hill, 2006.

Dean, Peter J., with Molly D. Shepard and Monica L. Warner. *The Coachable Leader: What Future Executives Need to Know Today.* Bloomington, IN: iUniverse, 2011.

Delaat, Jacqueline. *Gender in the Workplace: A Case Study Approach.* Thousand Oaks, CA: Sage, 2007.

Deluca, Joel R. *Political Savvy: Systematic Approaches to Leadership behind the Scenes.* Berwyn, PA: Evergreen Business Group, 1999.

Evans, Gail. *Play Like a Man, Win Like a Woman: What Men Know about Success That Women Need to Learn.* New York: Broadway, 2000.

Feiner, Michael. *The Feiner Points of Leadership: The 50 Basic Laws That Will Make People Want to Perform Better for You.* New York: McGraw-Hill, 2004.

Ferrazzi, Keith. *Never Eat Alone: And Other Secrets to Success, One Relationship at a Time.* New York: Doubleday, 2005.

Finkelstein, Sydney. *Why Smart Executives Fail.* New York: Portfolio, 2003.

Fisher, Donna. *Professional Networking for Dummies.* New York: Hungry Minds, 2001.

Fisher, Donna, and Sandy Vilas. *Power Networking: 59 Secrets for Personal and Professional Success.* Austin, TX: Bard Press, 2000.

Fisher, Helen. *The First Sex: The Natural Talents of Women and How They Are Changing the World.* New York: Random House, 1999.

Frankel, Lois. *Nice Girls Don't Get the Corner Office: 101 Unconscious Mistakes Women Make That Sabotage Their Careers.* New York: Warner Business, 2004.

Giovagnoli, Melissa, and Jocelyn Carter-Miller. *Networlding: Building Relationships and Opportunities for Success*. San Francisco: Jossey-Bass, 2000.

Gladwell, Malcolm. *The Tipping Point: How Little Things Can Make a Big Difference*. New York: Little, Brown, 2000.

Goleman, Daniel. *Emotional Intelligence: Why It Can Matter More Than IQ*. New York: Bantam, 1995.

Govindarajan, Vijay, and Chris Trimble. *Ten Rules for Strategic Innovators: From Idea to Execution*. Boston: Harvard Business School Press, 2005.

Gray, John. *Men Are from Mars, Women Are from Venus: The Classic Guide to Understanding the Opposite Sex*. New York: HarperCollins, 2004.

Hankin, Harriet. *The New Workforce: Five Sweeping Trends That Will Shape Your Company's Future*. New York: AMACOM, 2004.

Heenan, David, and Warren Bennis. *Co-Leaders: The Power of Great Partnerships*. New York: Wiley, 1999.

Holmes, Janet. *Gendered Talk at Work: Constructing Gender Identity through Workplace Discourse*. Oxford, UK, Blackwell, 2006.

Johnson, Tory, and Robyn Freedman Spizman. *Women for Hire's Get-Ahead Guide to Career Success*. New York: Berkley, 2004.

Jones, Charisse, and Kumea Shorter Gooden. *Shifting: The Double Lives of Black Women in America*. New York: HarperCollins, 2003.

Kantor, Roseabeth Moss. *Confidence: How Winning Streaks and Losing Streaks Begin and End*. New York: Crown, 2004.

Katzenbach, Jon R., Frederick Beckett, and Christopher Gagnon. *Real Change Leaders: How You Can Create Growth and High Performance at Your Company*. New York: Random House, 1995.

Kellerman, Barbara. *Bad Leadership: What It Is, How It Happens, Why It Matters*. Boston: Harvard Business School Press, 2004.

Kepcher, Carolyn, and Stephen Fenichell. *Carolyn 101: Business Lessons from The Apprentice's Straight Shooter*. New York: Fireside, 2004.

Klaus, Peggy. *Brag: The Art of Tooting Your Own Horn without Blowing It*. New York: Warner Books, 2003.

Kleiner, Art. *Who Really Matters: The Core Group Theory of Power, Privilege, and Success*. New York: Currency Doubleday, 2003.

Kofodimos, Joan R. *Balancing Act: How Managers Can Integrate Successful Careers and Fulfilling Personal Lives*. San Francisco: Jossey-Bass, 1993.

Kolb, Deborah M., Judith Williams, and Carol Frohlinger. *Her Place at the Table: A Woman's Guide to Negotiating Five Key Challenges to Leadership Success*. New York: Wiley, 2004.

Kolb, Deborah, and Judith Williams. *The Shadow Negotiation: How Women Can Master the Hidden Agendas That Determine Bargaining Success.* New York: Simon & Schuster, 2000.

Kouzes, James M., and Barry Z. Posner. *Credibility: How Leaders Gain and Lose It, Why People Demand It.* San Francisco: Jossey-Bass, 1995.

———. *The Leadership Challenge: How to Keep Getting Extraordinary Things Done in Organizations.* San Francisco: Jossey-Bass, 1995.

Lichtenberg, Ronna. *Pitch Like a Girl: How a Woman Can Be Herself and Still Succeed.* Emmaus, PA: Rodale, 2005.

Livers, Ancella B., and Keith A. Caver. *Leading in Black and White: Working across the Racial Divide in Corporate America.* New York: Wiley, 2002.

Loden, Marilyn. *Implementing Diversity: Best Practices for Making Diversity Work in Your Organization.* New York: McGraw-Hill, 1995.

Maxwell, John C. *The 21 Indispensable Qualities of a Leader: Becoming the Person Others Will Want to Follow.* New York: Thomas Nelson, 1999.

Miller, Lee E., and Jessica Miller. *A Woman's Guide to Successful Negotiating: How to Convince, Collaborate, and Create Your Way to Agreement.* New York: McGraw-Hill, 2002.

Morrison, Terri, Conaway A. Wayne, and George A. Borden. *Kiss, Bow, or Shake Hands: How to Do Business in Sixty Countries.* Holbrook, MA: Adams Media, 1994.

Nanus, Burt, and Warren Bennis. *Strategies for Taking Charge.* New York: Harper Business, 1997.

Neff, Thomas J., and James M. Citrin. *Lessons from the Top.* New York: Doubleday, 1999.

Orenstein, Peggy. *Flux: Women on Sex, Work, Kids, Love, and Life in a Half-Changed World.* New York: Doubleday, 2000.

Pachter, Barbara. *When the Little Things Count . . . And They Always Count: 601 Essential Things That Everyone in Business Needs to Know.* New York: Marlowe, 2001.

———. *The Power of Positive Confrontation: The Skills You Need to Know to Handle Conflict at Work, Home and in Life.* New York: Marlowe, 2001.

Pachter, Barbara, and Marjorie Brody. *The Complete Business Etiquette Handbook.* New York: Prentice Hall, 1994.

Parks, Sharon Daloz. *Leadership Can Be Taught: A Bold Approach for a Complex World.* Boston: Harvard Business School Press, 2005.

Patterson, Kerry, Joseph Grenny, David Maxfield, Ron McMillan, and Al Switzler. *Influencer: The Power to Change Anything.* New York: McGraw-Hill, 2007.

Pinkley, Robin L., and Gregory B. Northcraft. *Get Paid What You're Worth: The Expert Negotiators' Guide to Salary and Compensation.* New York: St. Martin's, 2003.

Reardon, Kathleen. *The Secret Handshake: Mastering the Politics of the Business Inner Circle.* New York: Doubleday, 2002.

Ruderman, Marian N., and Patricia J. Ohlott. *Standing at the Crossroads: Next Steps for High Achieving Women.* San Francisco: Jossey-Bass, 2002.

Russo, J. Edward, and Paul J. Schoemaker. *Decision Traps: Ten Barriers to Brilliant Decision-Making and How to Overcome Them.* New York: Simon & Schuster, 1990.

Sandberg, Sheryl. *Lean In: Women, Work, and the Will to Lead.* New York: Knopf, 2013.

Schein, Edgar. *Organizational Culture and Leadership.* San Francisco: Jossey-Bass, 1992.

Schoen, Marc. *Your Survival Instinct Is Killing You: Retrain Your Brain to Conquer Fear, Make Better Decisions, and Thrive in the 21st Century.* New York: Hudson Street Press, 2013.

Senge, Peter. *The Fifth Discipline: The Art and Practice of the Learning Organization.* New York: Currency Doubleday, 1994.

Shepard, Molly Dickinson. *Stop Whining and Start Winning: 8 Surefire Ways for Women to Thrive in Business.* New York: Penguin, 2005.

Shepard, Molly D., with Susannah Cobb and Starla Crandall. *Preparing for Your Prime Time: A Woman Boomer's Guide to Retirement.* Xlibris, 2012.

Tanenbaum, Leora. *Catfight: Women and Competition.* New York: Seven Stories, 2002.

Tichy, Noel, and Eli B. Cohen. *The Leadership Engine: How Winning Companies Build Leaders at Every Level.* New York: Harper Business, 1997.

Vrato, Elizabeth. *The Counselors: Conversations with 18 Courageous Women Who Have Changed the World.* Philadelphia: Running Press, 2003.

Watkins, Michael. *The First 90 Days: Critical Success Strategies for New Leaders at All Levels.* Boston: Harvard Business School Press, 2003.

Whitney, Catherine. *Nine and Counting, the Women of the Senate.* New York: HarperCollins, 2000.

Williams, Dean. *Real Leadership: Helping People and Organizations Face Their Toughest Challenges.* San Francisco: Berrett-Koehler, 2005.

Zander, Rosamund Stone, and Benjamin Zander. *The Art of Possibility.* Boston: Harvard Business School Press, 2000.

Zichy, Shoya, and Bonnie Kellen. *Women and the Leadership Q: Revealing the Four Paths to Influence and Power.* New York: McGraw-Hill, 2000.

References

Brizendine, Louann. *The Female Brain*. New York: Morgan Road, 2006.

Grant Thorton. "Women in Business," in *International Business Report 2007: Global Overview*. 27–29. Grant Thorton International, 2007.

Kahn Wilson, Karen, and Steven Salee. "Use Your Head: Insights on the Differences between Women's and Men's Brains and What These Differences Don't Mean," *Women Lawyers Journal* 90, no. 4 (Summer 2005), 26–28.

The Leader's Edge Research. *Behavioral Shift of Senior Executive Women*, 2001.

———. *Executive Women of African Descent*, 2006.

———. *Survey of Executive Women*, 2000.

———. *Why Senior Executive Women Change Jobs*, 2002.

Lublin, JoAnn S. "Even Top Executives Could Use Mentors to Benefit Careers," *Wall Street Journal*, July 1, 2003, B1.

Reier, Sharon. "In Europe, Women Finding More Seats at the Table," *New York Times*, March 22, 2008, www.nytimes.com/2008/03/22/business/world business/22director.html?fta=y (accessed October 28, 2008).

Tannen, Deborah. *You Just Don't Understand: Women and Men in Conversation*. New York: William Morrow, 1990.

U.S. Bureau of the Census. *Women's History Month: March 2006*. Pub. no. CB06-FF.03-2. A Facts for Features release, prepared by the Public Information Office, Bureau of the Census. Washington, DC, February 22, 2006.

Wall Street Journal. "Business Plan Flaws Can Be Fatal," October 28, 2002.

About the Authors

MOLLY D. SHEPARD, MS, MSM, founder and president of The Leader's Edge, is a dynamic speaker, author, and community leader. Her Philadelphia-based organization is the foremost leadership development and coaching practice committed to the advancement of senior executive women. Previously, Molly was chairman, president and co-founder of Manchester Inc., one of the world's largest career development consulting firms. While leading Manchester, she designed an executive format for leaders in transition that became the standard model for the industry. She is the recipient of many industry and community awards and serves on numerous public and nonprofit boards of directors. She is a trailblazer in women's leadership and in navigating the upper echelons of senior management. In 2006, Molly received an honorary doctorate of humane letters from West Chester University.

JANE K. STIMMLER, MLS, has over twenty-five years of experience in business, specifically in strategic marketing planning and communications. She is co-founder and president of The Marketing Edge, a Philadelphia-based marketing consulting and communications firm that has pioneered marketing strategies for financial companies and professional services firms. She has held executive positions in the banking, accounting, and legal industries. She is a university instructor and teaches on the subjects of business communication, organizational politics, and gender differences in the workplace. She frequently writes and speaks on marketing and management subjects, and about women in business. Jane is a recognized thought leader on the topic of women's advancement. She and her husband make their home in the Philadelphia area.

PETER J. DEAN, MS, PhD, is founder and president of Leaders By Design, an international leadership development coaching firm for senior executive men. He has authored nine books, published numerous articles, consulted, coached, and lectured in thirteen countries, and is a sought-after speaker by Fortune 50 companies on the topics of leadership, ethics, change management, performance improvement, and communication. For fifteen years, Peter was a lecturer at The Wharton School of the University of Pennsylvania. Also, he has been on faculty at the University of Iowa, Penn State University, University of Tennessee, and Fordham University. He held the O. Alfred Granum Chair in management at The American College, Bryn Mawr, Pennsylvania, where he designed the master of science in management program with an emphasis in leadership in 2004.

Peter Dean and Molly Shepard are married to each other and are partners in business. They are parents of four children, two of whom live with them in Philadelphia, Pennsylvania.